D1133766

EMPTY

The Journey From Emptiness to Purpose

ELIZABETH CARTER

Copyright © 2023 by Elizabeth Carter

All rights reserved. Except as permitted under the U.S. Copyright Act of 1976, no part of this publication may be reproduced, distributed, or transmitted in any form or by any means, electronic or mechanical, or stored in a database or retrieval system without the prior written permission of the publisher.

Unless otherwise stated, scripture references taken from the King James Version. Public Domain.

Any internet addresses (websites, blogs, etc.) and telephone numbers in this book are offered as a resource. They are not intended in any way to be or imply endorsement.

ISBN: 979-8-9884376-0-4

Available on Amazon.com and other retail outlets

Compiled and Written by: Elizabeth Carter

Interior Design & Editing by: A Marie Creative Services

This book is based on and inspired by true events.
Some names, locations, and identifying characteristics
have been changed to protect the privacy of those depicted.

Table of Contents

Section III - Fantasy Vs. Reality

Epilogue
About the Author

Preface

To be EMPTY is to experience a void that can only be filled by the Creator, Himself. There is no other way to understand it. For years I dreamed of sharing my story, believing God has prepared those hungry for the details. It was my desire to answer some of the questions they may be asking themselves and speak to many situations they may be experiencing.

Before now, I have allowed the fear of failure to deter me from writing it. I was perplexed about how to put my thoughts in print. I knew the story all too well, but how was I to put it in the pages of a book? I spent a lot of time being concerned about things that didn't matter: *Is anyone interested in my story? What if I can't complete it?*

One night, I prepared to turn in for the night. I laid in bed for hours, trying to drift off to sleep, and NOTHING happened. I was awake hour after hour, and then daylight crept in. I was still not asleep. I continued to ponder so many things, and then my cell phone lit up. There, on my phone, was a text message with a scripture, "Come to me, all who labor and are heavy laden, and I will give you rest. Take my yoke upon you, and learn from me, for I am gentle and lowly in heart, and you will find rest for your souls. For my yoke is easy, and my burden is light," Matthew 11:28-30.

If that wasn't perfect timing, I don't know what is. That was just what I needed at the moment. Although I feel helpless and lost, because I know Jesus, I found hope in Him. Everything looked bleak, but it was simply a teaching moment, an opportunity to grow. At that moment, I began writing this book with God's guidance, remembering, "I can do all things through Christ who strengthens me," Philippians 4:13.

Introduction

Sometimes on our way somewhere, we can lose our way and end up nowhere. We may find ourselves lost and caught up in a mental prison of our own thoughts. Let's be clear: Delayed does not mean denied, even when we allow bad choices to hinder our growth with useless distractions and fear.

My life was a mystery I desperately wanted to solve, and my biggest decision to change came when wanting to die became far more attractive than fighting to live. I was at a crossroads. I had an emptiness inside that I couldn't seem to fill. It left me anxiously looking forward to something yet wondering what that something was.

As I stumbled with great uncertainty, I learned many lessons along the way. I learned that I had the power to change direction and get off the dead-end road to destruction. I realized I was not what I had been through or where I came from, and I discovered the power within me to transform my life while remaining grateful for the process to do so. I could finish my way and on my terms, and I found hope and healing in the process.

On this journey, I traded loss, abuse, neglect, betrayal, disappointment, and emptiness for self-love, motivation, and encouragement. This propelled me through a productive yet unfamiliar move from emptiness to purpose.

The intent and desire for sharing my story is not only to provide encouragement but to impact, empower, and enrich the lives of others through transparency.

To every little girl that grew up not knowing who she was or if she had an identity at all, to that young woman hoping love would be enough to secure her happily ever after, to that seasoned queen after all the years of marriage is still trying to decide if she should leave or stay; be prepared to laugh, cry, get angry, and yet remain hopeful.

During extended reflection on seasons past, glean what is needed for growth and release what is not. Use pain as a stepping stone to your best days, one step at a time, to the life you were created to live. And remember, you are not alone. Many of us have felt empty during our lives in some form or another. But just as I did, you too can have an extreme makeover from the inside out by looking in the mirror with honesty and transparency and, for the first time, posing the question: WHO AM I?

EMPTY

Section I

WHO
AM I?

The
Early Years

We come into the world as helpless infants, completely dependent on parents we didn't choose. We find ourselves at their mercy for our every need. Our birth also begins a life-long journey of discovery. We begin by learning what it takes to get what we want.

When babies cry, it prompts action. When they are hungry, they cry. When they are wet, they cry. When they are uncomfortable, they cry. In most cases, crying works, and they are successful in getting their needs met.

Babies are also easily impressionable, and habits are developed early in life. They do what they see and repeat what they hear. More often than not, what is learned is good, but there are instances when bad habits are practiced and mastered, and this leads to more bad decisions.

Although we can't control how we start, good is attainable when we find the courage to overcome challenges and change what we don't like within.

The Joy of Food

Being born to a large family in the early '40s brought both joy and pain. As a baby, I was exceptional enough to have almost died due to starvation. Due to an allergic reaction to the formula I was drinking, I became malnourished and lost weight instead of gaining. This went unnoticed until a doctor pinpointed the problem nearly three months later.

Once discovered, I was prescribed a new type of infant formula. My first bottle of formula stayed down, even after the burp. It left me nice and full. However, my stomach began to protrude as though I had blown up a balloon and swallowed it whole. This potbelly left me with a lifelong reminder of my struggle to survive.

I'm told feeding time was my favorite time. It started with the new formula, and as I grew older, my love for food continued. We had excellent cooks in our family, and every celebration included good food and plenty of it. No matter the occasion, good or bad, food made everything beautiful, one meal at a time.

During my adolescent years, Saturday was my favorite day of the week. Waking up to the smell of great food was a joy. The breakfast menu was filled with whatever your heart desired... *and I mean everything.* The pancakes were large enough to fill the plate: tender, fluffy, and covered with butter. They were soft all the way through and never gooey. The scrambled eggs were cooked perfectly, not runny or dry, and were complemented with baked biscuits from scratch, covered with freshly churned butter dripping over them. Now, you may be thinking, *both pancakes and biscuits?* Yes, and both covered with delicious Brer Rabbit Syrup. Let's not forget the meats: crispy bacon, links, and sausage, browned to perfection with a bit of gravy on the side, along with grits cooked with butter and sugar.

Weekly dinners included items I still love today: turnip greens, hot water corn bread, candied yams, and salmon croquettes with baked beans. Well, you get the point.

Barbecues were also a special treat. Saturated with an underlying smokiness, the brisket was so tender it could be eaten with a spoon. The meat on the ribs would fall off the bone and slide right into your mouth. It was paired with potato salad and grilled beans for a mouthwatering combination. The meat needed no sauce, but the homemade barbecue sauce was great for dipping bread. It was so finger-licking good that no towel was required. I didn't want to miss a bite.

Mealtimes brought us joy, and every dish was perfect without fail. The phrase "eat, drink, and be merry" was a reminder of the beginning of my love-hate relationship with food. This major contributor would impact my life for years to come and served as a constant reminder of why we moved to that house.

Esther

My parents, Jane and Roger, were young when they married, children having children. My father was a hard-working man, but because my mother's job was to be a housewife and mother, we moved often and even lived with relatives at times. Nevertheless, we were happy as long as we were together. A baby was born approximately every ten months, resulting in nine babies born in nine years, although not all survived. In total, there were five surviving children, which weighed heavily on our family budget and the ability to keep up with everything required to run a home without assistance.

Growing up in a large family posed its own set of challenges. My siblings and I quickly learned to share everything, including gifts during Christmas time. Typically, we would get gifts that we could all play with. However, there was one Christmas I remember extremely well. This was the Christmas I received my first doll. I was so excited. I finally had something of my own, and she was the first something I could finally connect with. I named her Esther, taken from the television show Sanford and Son.

My siblings talked about how ugly she was, and it was good they thought so because nobody wanted to play with her. She was tall with long black hair, and she came with one plain yellow dress. She was beautiful to me, and I carried her with me everywhere I went. I spent my days combing her hair and changing that one dress, pretending she had a wardrobe with a different outfit each time.

I kept Esther for years, up until we went on a road trip to visit relatives. Their family was larger than ours, and they lived on fifty acres of land in a small country town a few hours away. There was so much to do at their house, and we had a blast. We rode horses, swam in the lake, and made up random games to play. It was a joyous time and the only time I forgot about my little doll.

As we ended our week-long trip and began packing to leave, I could not find Esther. Everybody looked for Esther, but we couldn't find her. I was sure I brought her along because Esther and I enjoyed the long ride together. Sadly, I would not take her back home. I believe one of my cousins kept her, but I could never prove it.

You may ask, *What was so special about this doll?* Esther was the one thing I could call my own. I was attached to her and told her all my secrets.

Living in a Fantasy

As a young girl, I often thought I was adopted and never seemed to fit in. I didn't favor any of my siblings or share any apparent qualities that would have helped me feel at ease. So, I learned to cope with the life I had been given by creating an alter ego who lived in a fantasy world. Her name was Sandy, and Esther was her best friend. They were the dynamic duo, and I didn't have to compete with anyone for her attention. Everyone in my present world was excluded from visiting my place of refuge, except for Esther. She would never be replaced.

I was always grateful to my mother for buying me this doll, which allowed me to create this fantasy world. The fondest memories of my mother include Esther since she was always with me during my childhood. Although we were in constant chaos, we had fun times and enjoyed the lives we had.

A Million Dollar Smile

My mother was carefree and playful. She loved music, dancing, and, of course, affection. In looking at how the family increased every year, it seemed her other favorite thing to do was to be intimate with my father.

My mother was a beautiful woman with a million-dollar smile, pearly white teeth, long black curly hair, and pretty milk chocolate skin. Her smile could take your breath away, and she was gorgeous inside and out. Not to mention, her high-caliber personality could fill any empty space. She loved to have a good time. She was the life of the party, pregnant or not. If an event was not *lit* before she arrived, it would be once she stepped into the room.

Although my mother was fun, she was a firecracker as well. If you rolled up on her or anyone she cared for, she could pop off at any time. She wasn't afraid of anything and would fight in a minute, but she lived life to the fullest and never let anyone or anything get her down.

Visiting the Farm

Shortly after my last sibling was born, my mother made the decision to shut down the baby factory. She did not want to have any additional children and decided to explore her options for birth control.

On this particular day, she informed us that we were going to spend a few days with our favorite cousins because she had some business to take care of. We had become accustomed to staying a few days away from home, usually when a new addition to the family was expected. However, we knew that was not the case this time because she didn't have the big stomach she had during previous times.

As children, we went with the flow. We loved going to the country to visit our Aunt Edith and our Uncle Jimmy. We could run around outside and play, and some days, we actually caught our dinner, which included what they raised on the farm. I loved to fetch eggs in the morning before breakfast. However, I never liked catching chickens. I believed that task should have been left for the boys, not the girls. I also learned how to milk a cow and churn butter. At their house, there was nothing but laughter, good food, and fun memories.

Jimmy and Edith were great people, and they loved us. They made us feel at home every time, treating us just as they treated their own children. Edith was a fabulous cook. Although she was known for her famous peach cobbler, there wasn't anything she didn't cook, and every dish was made from scratch. She was both a mother and a housewife and, oftentimes, helped to keep the farm along with her husband, Jimmy, who looked to be about seven feet tall and three hundred pounds. Jimmy was a giant teddy bear who loved children. He worked the farm and held a job as well, but whenever they had visitors, he and his wife partnered as the perfect hosts.

The Day Everything Changed

This visit turned out to be different from any other visit in more ways than one. Little did we know, it would be one we could never forget. This visit will go down in history as the day when everything changed.

We woke up to a beautiful day. The sun shined brightly in our eyes, hitting at least 80 degrees on that hot day in August. After breakfast, we went out to play, staying out for hours. We even ate sandwiches outside for lunch. When we got hot and thirsty, we ran to the well and drew some water to quench our thirst. The well was deep, with access to groundwater drawn up manually with a bucket. Nothing beats cool, delicious water from a well. It's so crisp and clear. After the sun went down, it was time to go in and wash up for dinner.

When we entered the house, the atmosphere had changed. For the first time ever, there were no smiles and not an ounce of joy was felt. It seemed that the sadness had come while we were out playing. We couldn't understand the mood as children, but we did notice the difference.

There was no dinner on the table or anyone in the kitchen preparing dinner. No one said a word, other than the directive to go get washed up for dinner. The puzzling thing was there was no dinner to wash up for. At that moment, nothing made sense. Yet, in those days, children were seen and not heard in our family. You did what you were told to do and don't speak unless you're spoken to. No questions allowed. The adults' favorite saying was, *Learn to stay out of grown folks' business.* However, we thought it was our business because we were hungry and wanted to know when we could eat, but we did as we were told. We washed up, sat down, and played games inside the house until we were told dinner was ready.

Alone

We later learned that our mother, Jane, had decided to speak with a doctor about how to be intimate without having children. At the time, not being intimate was not a viable option. She contacted her mother, whom we called Mommie Dearest, and told her of her plans. Mommie Dearest was unable to make it to the appointment, but our mother was unwilling to reschedule and proceeded to the visit alone.

Jane was stubborn, headstrong, and impatient. She did what she wanted no matter what. Our mother went to the appointment alone, made the decision to have a tubal ligation, and scheduled a date for surgery. When the day came, she chose to go alone again, and the doctor performed the procedure.

Soon after the surgery, she caught an infection, which caused her to have a high fever. Because she was somewhat out of it, the hospital began to notify her emergency contacts and request their presence at the hospital. They were unable to reach our father, so they contacted her second emergency contact, her mother, and asked her to come as soon as possible. Mommie Dearest quickly headed to the hospital, her mind racing with all types of thoughts and scenarios about what was going on with her daughter as she made the twenty-minute drive.

Upon arrival, she immediately requested to speak to the doctor. She was advised they were attempting to treat the infection, but they had not been successful up to that point. They assured her they were still trying to treat the infection and reduce her fever, and per their policy, they thought it best to call family to be with her.

Mommie Dearest visited for hours until our father arrived. Then, she made her way to us.

Mommie Dearest walked into Jimmy and Edith's home with a somber look on her face, barely acknowledging any of the children. Eventually, dinner was served, and the mood lightened a bit.

As we ate dinner, the adults talked in another part of the house. We didn't hear the conversation, but we knew something was amiss. They soon ended their conversation, and Mommie Dearest prepared to leave. She stopped by the table to say goodbye and tell us that she had brought additional clothes because we would be staying for a few more days. She did not say one word about our mother being ill and in the hospital.

This day became a game changer for me and my siblings. As I reflect on this particular day, I realize just how much it impacted me. I was too young to know it then, but this would be the start of the patterns that shaped me. How I thought, my reactions, my insecurities, and my choices would forever be impacted by this moment in time. The question, "*Who am I*," would be a question that haunted me through years of pain, heartache, and struggle to come.

When my mother decided she no longer wanted to have children, she believed the surgery was her best option. She told those closest to her that she wanted to have the procedure done and get it over with so she could move on with her life. She took the doctor's advice and didn't feel she needed anyone else to help her sort out the best option. She lived her life on a fast track. So it was not uncommon for her to make decisions in haste. However, this time, things would not turn out as she had planned. She would not get the chance to move on with her life as she thought. A few days later, she passed quietly due to complications from the operation. Her cause of death was listed as an embolism to the heart.

Many believed the doctor was negligent and the hospital was unsanitary, but that was just hearsay. It was never proven. However, no one could make sense of this situation. A young, healthy woman with no underlying health conditions walks into a hospital for a minor procedure, and less than a week later, she leaves in a box, deceased. Instead of going on with her life as she had hoped, she lost her life, and plans for her funeral began.

Gone but Not Forgotten

We remained with our cousins while all of the funeral arrangements were handled. We knew something was wrong, but we were too young to understand why a typically jovial home was now sad and dark.

Although memories of my mother are few, the day of her funeral sticks out in my mind as though it was yesterday. It was held in a small church with standing room only. People from near and far came to support the family and give their condolences.

The casket spray was filled with several assorted colors and looked like a beautiful rainbow. The service continued for hours on that long, sad day. When the minister finished the eulogy, he beckoned for the mortuary staff to come. They lifted the lid of the casket slowly and prepared for the final viewing.

As they placed the spray on the other end of the casket, they handled a few final touches before calling up the first group.

As my mother lay there, beautiful as ever, as if she were sleeping, each attendee viewed her angelic face one last time. I watched as they stopped at her casket with tear-filled eyes and full of grief, reminiscing on all the memories they shared with her and great sadness over the fact that there would be no new ones. I heard expressions of regret, some saying how they wished things were different and others wanting to be anywhere but there, celebrating her young life.

My mother was thirty years young. Gone but never forgotten, her memory living on in the hearts of all who love her. She left this earth filled with the potential of what she could have been. We, her children, were sad and lost and had no concept of what all of this meant for us.

The time had come for the service to end. As everyone departed and traveled back to their respective lives, we didn't know what to think or do as we sat bewildered, confused, anxious, dumbfounded, and curious about where we would go from there. At the time, we did not understand that would be the last time we would see our mother, other than in a picture frame.

The funeral thing was new and unfamiliar, but there was a lingering sense of sadness that never quite disappeared. In fact, I had an emptiness and void that remained with no clear understanding of how to fill it. I still feel that sense of sadness when I think of my mother today. I also wonder how differently my life might have turned out if she had lived. *Would it be better or worse? Would I be happy or sad? Would there be lack or plenty?* Either way, there will never be the opportunity to ask her life-changing questions with answers only she could provide.

That House

Early on, our grandparents on both sides were active in our lives and pitched in whenever necessary when a new arrival came into the family. Mommie Dearest did everything she could to help my mother and was always there for her. Because of their close relationship, it is easy to understand that when my mother died, a part of Mommie Dearest died with her. She never grieved outwardly. Instead, she suppressed it, leaving her bitter, sad, and filled with regret. Mentally and psychologically incapacitated, Mommie Dearest remained in a state of shock and denial after the funeral and tried to move on with life as though it had never happened.

She didn't realize she had a problem. So her grief was never addressed. Admitting there was a problem would force her to lose control, and that could never happen. She refused to admit that she needed anything from anyone, and this character flaw eventually turned into rage.

My mother's deathbed request was to keep her children together. So, we were to pack up and move in with Mommie Dearest. My mother believed this was best for us, and my father accepted the plan. He left the funeral that day devastated, numb, and alone. What he did know was that he would not take his children home with him that day. What he didn't know was that he would remain estranged from us for several years afterward.

Not only was that our last day to see our mother and father, but it was also the day we learned life as we knew it was about to change. The only place we knew as home was gone, and our happy days were over. We didn't know what to expect, but one thing was clear: good or bad, this was our new life.

My father later learned that was not the best decision, but this fact would remain a secret for years to come. He had no idea what we would endure behind closed doors.

Section II

BEHIND CLOSED DOORS

Change
is Inevitable

The years spent with Mommie Dearest were quite different from what I had grown accustomed to. One early morning incident served as a wake-up call of just how much things would change.

I was sleeping soundly in my bed when all of a sudden, I heard, "Wake up! Get up before I knock you out of that bed! I mean get up RIGHT NOW and come to the kitchen."

I slowly sat up, matted eyes and all. Confused, I began stretching my arms and yawning. In an attempt to open my eyes, I began to rub them. Right at that moment, I felt a slap on my head, "Get yo' butt up, girl, and I am NOT going to tell you again!"

My eyes opened wide. Scared, shaking, and sweating, I tried to figure out what was going on. I followed Mommie Dearest to the kitchen, at which time she asked, "What did I tell you about going to bed without washing these dishes?" I attempted to explain to her that I did clean the entire kitchen before I went to bed, "I swear I did." She said, "Stop lying and get in that bathroom right now!"

I hesitantly walked to the bathroom, and she followed close behind. As soon as we entered, she closed the door and told me to "strip." I looked at her, frozen in place, with tears rolling down my face. I was in total shock. With my lips quivering, I softly asked, "Ma'am?" She said, "You heard me. Did I stutter? Take those clothes off! Every piece! And get down on your knees and hug that bathtub."

I slowly unbuttoned my top...really slow...one button at a time. I was still shaking, fingers barely able to push the button through the hole. First one, second one, third one, and then I had an idea. I said I needed to pee in an attempt to buy some time. Maybe she'll come to her senses. I really did have to pee, and I was so nervous that it wasn't all I had to do.

She said, "Girl, I don't have all night. I'm tired. Now, stop faking and get over here!" Finally, with the last button undone, my pajamas fell, and I stood there in nothing but my birthday suit. I got down on my knees and began hugging the bathtub with all my might, just as she instructed.

I sat in that position for what seemed like an hour as she told me how much she loved me. She explained that she was doing this because of love and said she was not going to allow me to be hardheaded like my mother. She continued by saying, "And when I tell you to do something, you better do it and do it exactly like I said. Do you hear me?" I respond, "Yes, Ma'am," thinking, *Whatever this is, can we just get it over with so I can go back to bed?*

I thought I was prepared for what would come next, but I was sorely mistaken. The first lick came, right across my back, hard and intentional. It was so hard that I felt the skin break on my back. I screamed out, "O-U-C-H!" and started crying. I felt like I was about to die! There was no time to breathe or recover before another one came, then another, and another. I wasn't sure how long it lasted, but it felt like forever.

I screamed out in pain with every lash until she said, "Shut up before you wake the others." I thought to myself, *How do I shut up when you are literally performing surgery on my back without anesthesia?* As I felt the blood running down my back, I made the mistake of putting my arm up as a defense. What did I do that for! Now my arm was catching the licks as well.

The beating went on so long that I began to notice a rhythm to the hits. They got harder and quicker each time, as though she was beating me to the rhythm of a drum or a chord of music in a song. The strange thing was it seemed almost as if she liked it.

When she finally finished, she said, "Clean up that blood and get in there and clean the kitchen. If this happens again, it will be worse next time." Weak and in pain, I attempted to stand, but my legs didn't help much. They were limp.

I went into deep thought, thinking, *How can I get away from here?* I felt all alone with no one to help me. As I sat in tears with my nose running, she interrupted my thoughts and said, "Girl, if you don't get up and clean this mess right now – or do you want some more?" I quickly replied, "No, Ma'am."

My legs suddenly grew strong at the thought of more. As I cleaned up the blood from what seemed like the entire bathroom, Mommie Dearest turned to me and said, "I only do this because I love you." I thought, *Could you please hate me instead? If this is your idea of love, I want no part of it.*

A New Normal

The fan belt's intended purpose is to keep the fan running under the hood of a car. Generally, when that belt breaks, it is thrown in the trash. But not in this case. That fan belt is what was used to punish me and my siblings.

It has been suggested that this is how Mommie Dearest's generation was punished. She was raised "in the old days," when they were expected to just get over it. If she was beaten to the point that every lick cut her skin and blood had to be cleaned up afterward, why would she want to pass that on to her children and grandchildren? I don't think I'll ever understand that. We were her only daughter's children, and I don't know how she could sleep at night knowing the abusive environment she created.

After cleaning the bathroom and the kitchen, I had this great idea a bath would possibly help with the pain. I figured warm water and Epsom salt always make sore muscles feel better. Maybe it would work on this too. WOW, was I wrong! As I slowly sat in the bathwater, the pain was excruciating. I put a towel in my mouth to muffle my scream. I quickly jumped up and rethought my plan.

Realizing I needed to somehow sit down in the water, I decided to slowly ease my body in and slide into the water. It took a few attempts before I could sit down in it. The salted water eventually made my back feel better, but it would take weeks to heal from that awful beating.

It seemed like this was some kind of sick welcome-home party. I could have never anticipated this new normal.

The times with Mommie Dearest were very traumatic. Nobody could help us because no one knew what we endured at the hands of Mommie Dearest.

For some reason or another, these beatings would happen monthly. I learned there was no way to avoid them because there was no rhyme or reason for them. It wasn't the big things that provoked the beatings. They happened whenever, however, and for whatever reason she deemed appropriate.

With no method to the madness, it was almost like the rules were made up along the way. Mommie Dearest was mad at the world, but the world didn't live with her; we did. By no means were we perfect, but the punishment never fit the crime. This had become our everyday life, and since we had nothing more than vague memories to compare it to, we grew up believing it was normal.

Beauty is Only Skin Deep

The physical abuse was horrible, but the mental and verbal was worse. For instance, if a stranger told me I was pretty, Mommie Dearest would quickly tell me, "Don't believe that nonsense. They are just trying to make you feel good. They just feel sorry for you 'cause you are so ugly." After being told this so many times, I started to believe it. I didn't understand the difference between what I saw in the mirror and what others saw in me. I took her words as truth, believing she was an expert on good looks.

Mommie Dearest was a beautiful woman with an inviting smile and pearly white teeth. She was petite with smooth, caramel-brown skin absent of any discolorations. She had long, naturally straight, dark hair with a hint of salt and pepper, which she wore in a bun. She had a conservative look, a perfectionist that never lost control. The best inspector could visit her home any time, day or night, and she would pass the white glove test. Her home was spotless, not a general clean but brand new clean, with no exception. If it wasn't spotless at all times, there would be hell to pay.

Mommie Dearest owned her own catering business for over fifty years. She was the best in her trade, and people drove from miles around to receive her services. She was a bit slow, but her clients did not seem to mind because every creation was perfect every time. She was an extraordinarily talented person, yet quiet and soft-spoken. She knew what she wanted, and everything she touched was successful. Every goal she created for herself was achieved.

Like Mother, Like Daughter

Sadly, the one thing Mommie Dearest could not control was the death of her daughter, her only child. Jane was the apple of her eye, her pride and joy. There was nothing too good for her daughter. Needless to say, she was spoiled. In fact, some could say she was disobedient. The day she went to see the surgeon alone against her mother's request could be considered evidence of this disobedience.

I often wondered if things would have turned out differently had she waited for her mother. The truth about spoiling children is there are no boundaries, and sometimes that is the very thing required to guide them in the right direction.

She loved my mother in a way mere words can't describe, and when she died, it seemed Mommie Dearest's ability to love died as well. But did it?

My eldest sister, Janice, had lived with Mommie Dearest since the day she was born. Jane and Janice were considered Mommie Dearest's "first two girls," and they were viewed as the same person in her eyes. They were allowed to get away with everything, and because of that, they didn't always make good decisions. Mommie Dearest vowed she would not make the same mistake with the last three girls. We would be punished severely before we ever had the chance to make wrong choices.

After my mother's death, Mommie Dearest directed her affection to Janice and treated her as though she was her only daughter. Because of this, the two had a bond that was never allowed to flow to me and my other siblings. It felt like Mommie Dearest punished the rest of us because we lived and her daughter died.

Things Are Not Always As They Appear

What was most disturbing is Mommie Dearest was highly respected in her neighborhood and community. She was viewed as a hero for raising her daughter's children after her death. Yet no one realized how little they really knew about this woman with multiple personalities.

Mommie Dearest always made sure we were dressed to impress, no matter where we went. Many believed we had a much better life with my grandmother than we would've had if our young mother had lived. However, one thing is true: Things are not always as they appear. Evil hides in many homes, behind closed doors, where secrets stay hidden for years. Money is no replacement for decency and love, but it often hides signs and symptoms that would be otherwise evident.

For example, if a child shows up at school wearing torn, dirty clothes, smelling like they have not had a bath in days, someone would notice that child and investigate further. Now, let's say another child shows up to school wearing expensive clothes and has every hair in place. They would rarely receive the same attention. In this example, both are being neglected, but only one receives the attention to prompt the necessary assistance they need.

On many occasions, we were instructed to take notes to school with various reasons as to why we could not dress for Physical Education. No matter how many notes we took, the teachers accepted the note every time, no questions asked. The reality is that if we had dressed out, all the bruises would be visible, and the secret would be out.

Mommie Dearest needed psychological help to deal with her only daughter's death and care for five small children affected by that same death. If just one person had noticed the problem or her husband would have anonymously reported it, we could have avoided years of abuse. Sometimes people look, but they refuse to see the subtle hints or mannerisms of children crying out for help. Those cries go ignored because people don't want to get involved. It has been said it takes a village to raise a child, but in this case, the village failed us and our grandmother.

My Fantasy World

After receiving the beatings for years, I began to convince myself it was not me being hit. My alter ego, Sandy, slowly exited her fantasy world and entered my version of hell. I began spending more and more time in my fantasy world. My mind had helped me escape my reality. I would spend day after day pretending that I lived in a loving home and had a wonderful life. Fantasizing about being like my cousins with two loving parents in an environment where positive encouragement and love were evident made life bearable. It was always happy there. It was a place I never wanted to leave, unlike my home.

Once I found Sandy again, I was able to escape when it was time for a beating. I would no longer cry because Sandy was being hit, not me. Oh, did this upset Mommie Dearest. The first time it happened, Mommie Dearest was so mad! But I secretly enjoyed it. In my mind, I was winning.

As she commenced with the beating, she repeated, "So, you not gon' cry, huh?" Seeing she wasn't going to get the result she wanted, she stopped, rested, and came back a second time. Then, a third. Sandy still wouldn't cry. Mommie Dearest was furious. It was as if she realized that she had lost control. She no longer had the joy of seeing me cry.

This tactic worked so well that I transitioned into my fantasy world full-time. Pretending was far better than my real life. I dreamed about the day I could leave Mommie Dearest's house and never go back.

The Great Escape

A few months after escaping to my fantasy world, another incident would push me over the edge. One afternoon, one of my grandmother's customers came by to pick up an order. She began to share some neighborhood gossip, which included me and my cousin's husband. Of course, it wasn't true, but Mommie Dearest didn't like anything that made her look like she didn't have control of her household.

She later confronted me, and I told her it was a lie, but that didn't matter. After asking a few more times, the beating began. She continued to ask me what happened between my cousin's husband and me, and I stood firm on my answer, "Nothing! Nothing happened!" After realizing she would never accept the truth, I decided to lie. I told her what I thought she wanted to hear, but that didn't work either. She then started beating me for lying to her in the first place. I didn't know what to do. She beat me until I said I did it, and then beat me because I said I did it. I was in a lose-lose situation.

As I cleaned myself up, I decided I couldn't stay there anymore. I decided to run away, but I didn't have a plan. No money, no clothes, and no destination. I just wanted out.

That evening, we ate dinner with Grandpa Robert, as usual. I knew Mommie Dearest was in for the night, and Grandpa Robert would be right behind her. I slowly did my chores that night, waiting until the house was settled, and then I made my great escape.

I figured I'd head in the direction of my father's house, and when I got there, I would tell him what was going on. I still had fresh wounds to prove it. I thought maybe he could be the one to rescue us from the hell we were in.

I walked for what seemed like hours when a highway patrolman spotted me. He took one look at me and realized he knew me. In looking at the time, he knew I was not supposed to be out by myself and marched me straight home and right into the hands of Mommie Dearest.

Once I got home, I got it good, both for running away and embarrassing Mommie Dearest. That was the worst beating of all. Even in the fantasy world, I never tried that again. Instead, I chose to focus on getting through school. That would be my official way out. Mommie Dearest had one rule: If you want to leave, graduate from high school. So, I made that my goal.

A Ray of Sunshine

Grandpa Robert was a gentle, loving man who served as a ray of sunshine in that house of hell. No one would believe he was not our biological grandfather because he did all he could to bring us joy, but his power was limited.

Most days, he was treated just like one of the children, and it was difficult to understand why he would let his wife treat him that way. He was talked down to and disrespected, and all he would do was drop his head with a look of defeat on his face. The disappointment and hopelessness was evident, especially when it came to us.

As children, we were all close. So, when one of us was getting beat, we would all cry. In an attempt to calm those of us who were not being punished, Grandpa Robert would take us for a ride. There were also times when he would step in and take a few licks for us in an attempt to get her to stop. He would allow her rage to be put on him to give us a reprieve every now and then, but he could not stop the beatings. Grandpa Robert loved Mommie Dearest in a way many could never understand. I believe deep down, he wanted to get help for us, but the only way he could do that was to betray his wife, and that was something he never had the heart to do.

Grandpa Robert was an excellent cook. Because he worked long hours during the week, the weekends and holidays were the highlight for us. We knew there would always be something good to look forward to. His food made our mouths and stomachs happy. When he served breakfast, lunch, or dinner, our world was transformed. He believed in making sure everyone had plenty to eat, and his meals left everyone completely satisfied and almost miserably full. Grandpa Robert showed his love through cooking because he knew it made us smile, and he did it well. He loved to fish. That was his form of relaxation to get away from it all.

My grandpa was a hard-working man. So when he decided he would retire from his job after twenty-plus years to spend more time with family and fish, it seemed like happy days were coming soon. He announced his retirement while we were in high school, and we were all looking forward to it.

More Ways of Escape

I was responsible for cleaning the kitchen daily, and I enjoyed this most on Saturday mornings. After Saturday morning breakfast, I was able to clean up while listening to the radio. After completing my chores, I would escape to my fantasy world, where Sandy would play the piano and makeup songs to sing.

I truly enjoyed singing. Music made me smile, and I could connect through song in a way most could never imagine. I had a soft voice and sang soprano, and I must say, I could sing well. Mommie Dearest even allowed me to sing in the church choir and throughout the community.

I also used school as another way of escape. My high school years presented both good and bad times, but I made the best of it. Because of my horrific home life, I poured myself into the classes I loved and found several distractions at school. Bringing home failing grades was not allowed, and I tried my hardest not to interrupt the perception of perfection. However, that would only last for a short while until I disappointed Mommie Dearest again, just as I always seemed to do.

And You Say He's Just a Friend

At age fourteen, I noticed boys because they noticed me. I was a shy young lady, but I was happy someone was giving me some attention. My social skills were not the best, and the first couple of boyfriends I had did not work out so well, but that was no surprise as I had no relationship skills or knowledge about anything of substance in that area.

The summer before my sophomore year, I had become really good friends with a girl named Tasha. Soon after, her cousin Javier moved in with her so he could transfer to our school. Javier was extraordinarily handsome and dressed like he had just stepped out of Hollywood. He was confident, yet shy, with the most beautiful brown eyes, and his smile could melt a block of ice. I secretly invited him into my fantasy world since that was the only place I thought he would give me the time of day. I figured it didn't hurt to dream.

When the school year started, I walked into class, and there he was. I thought I was going to faint. Because he was new and I was friends with his cousin, we got acquainted pretty quickly. We eventually became partners in crime from a friendship perspective. I couldn't wait to get to school every day to talk to him. He was soft-spoken, and it seemed like he knew everything. He was also a good listener. I don't think either of us focused completely on the class during those days, but the teacher was pretty cool. As long as we did our work, he didn't mind.

Javier had a girlfriend, and I had a boyfriend at the time. So we spent a lot of time talking about them. We also shared plans for the weekend, as if I really had plans. He always had something interesting planned. So I pretended I had plans as well. After the semester ended, we remained friends and talked off and on. Eventually, our respective relationships ended, and our friendship transitioned into something neither of us had planned. It just happened.

By this time, it was the summer before my junior year and the summer before Javier's senior year. We hung out all summer when we weren't working. He loved to fish, and I welcomed any opportunity to get out of the house. I loved going with him and would sit under a tree and read. We enjoyed the quality time and learned a lot about each other. We shared our secrets, goals, and aspirations as we sat together and bonded. I couldn't imagine why he wanted to be with me. I saw myself as a plain, average girl with little knowledge about anything relevant. All I had to offer was a listening ear.

Javier was the exact opposite. He was very handsome. And did I mention his million-dollar smile and those beautiful brown eyes I loved to look into when he talked? Javier helped me through some extremely rough times during my high school years. He encouraged me through two complicated relationships and allowed me to cry on his shoulder when things were tough at home.

He also told me on many occasions that I was beautiful, which was difficult for me to accept. The girl he cared for was a girl I did not recognize. I believed something was wrong with me, and I felt ugly and worthless, a mindset that would follow me for years to come. I often thought, *This handsome guy could choose whatever girl he wanted. Why did he choose me?* The reality was we were two extraordinary people who viewed ourselves as simply ordinary. We could, in no way, anticipate the plan unfolding for our lives.

Mommie Dearest allowed me to date, but Javier was not someone she wanted me to be with. She said he was no good and that he didn't mean me any good. She didn't outright forbid it but was against it as soon as she learned whose child he was. Ironically, she loved his mother but not his father. She believed that because his father was no good, he must be no good too.

I desperately wanted Mommie Dearest to be wrong. Javier and I were best friends, and when I was with him, I felt like I was sitting on top of the world. We had fun together and were affectionate with one another, kissing and hugging as many young people do at that age. But there was no sex. Of course, the topic frequently came up in conversation, but that was all it was. Just talk. All I knew was this was my forever guy. As long as I was with him, everything would be okay. I did not have a clue that my thoughts would prove to be far from the truth.

The Big Step

The summer before my senior year, I chose to take the big step with Javier, against my better judgment. I had no clue what the big step included or the consequences that could result from that decision. When we did, I hated it! I wondered why anyone would want to do that. My inexperience and lack of knowledge left me with so many questions. My dilemma was I had no one to discuss this with. It was so awkward and embarrassing, and I knew it was wrong. I shouldn't have done it, but I wanted to prove to Javier that I really loved him. But I couldn't help but think, *Now what? Would he really want me to do that again?* He admitted that he didn't believe me when I said I was not sexually active, but I was obviously telling the truth.

As the days turned into weeks, I noticed that my breasts began to fill out, and my body was changing in a way I didn't understand. Mommie Dearest noticed it as well. My potbelly was looking a bit more bloated, even though I had lost a few pounds.

After about two months of noticing these changes, Mommie Dearest asked me point-blank if I was pregnant. I looked confused and baffled and immediately responded, No! After a few more weeks passed, Mommie Dearest asked again. I was clueless and thought to myself, *Why does she keep asking me that?* Since there had been no talk about sex, pregnancy, or even marriage, how was I supposed to know?

The following week, she took me to the doctor for a pregnancy test, and the results revealed I was pregnant, which baffled me. In my early teen years, I was told that I would never be able to have children because of a medical problem, but to my surprise, there I was...pregnant. Either the previous doctor didn't know what he was talking about, or this was a miracle. Either way, my grandmother was furious. When we returned home, I received the last beating of my life for lying about being pregnant.

The Aftermath

After that, life with Mommie Dearest got much worse. She went to a new level with her name-calling and put-downs, calling me a nasty whore, an embarrassment to the family, and a crazy fool. She also told me that Javier was sure to leave me and move on to someone else now that I was pregnant.

Javier and I had many discussions about marriage and what life could be like in the future, but we hadn't planned for any of it so soon. When I called Javier and told him I was pregnant, he, too, was shocked, scared, and confused. He immediately talked with his family because this pregnancy process was one thing neither of us knew anything about. His family encouraged him to do the right thing and marry me. However, I refused. Even though I had dreamed and fantasized about marrying him and living happily ever after, I did not want it to happen this way. I was confused and frustrated and needed time to process it all. I wondered, *How am I to prepare to be some child's mother when I am only a child myself?*

To say Grandpa Robert loved children was an understatement. He loved everybody's children and was supportive throughout my pregnancy. As much as Mommie Dearest made my life a living hell, Grandpa Robert was excited about the baby. He talked about wanting to babysit while I went to college and even said he was going to take the baby fishing with him when he retired.

I don't think I was prepared for how much my life would change after my pregnancy was confirmed. I was just beginning my senior year in high school when Mommie Dearest pulled me out of school and made me take classes from home. She was embarrassed and didn't want me out in public in any way.

My teachers were extremely disappointed as well. One of my favorite teachers pulled me aside to let me know just how disappointed she was by saying, "I would have never expected you to be one of those loose girls. You had so much potential, and now your life is ruined." These were words I would rehearse in my mind time and time again.

Because I was not in school, Mommie Dearest made me prepare meals for the customers of her catering business during my entire pregnancy. This was her way of punishing me for being pregnant. I guess she figured she might as well put me to work since I was no longer going to school every day.

Just when I thought things couldn't get any worse, when I was seven months pregnant, life would throw another stone our way that would shake up our world once again.

The Last Breakfast

Grandpa Robert woke up early one Saturday morning and prepared to cook breakfast. He was excited because he had plans to go fishing later that day. It was a few days before his birthday and his scheduled retirement, and he was excited to enjoy some time doing what he loved. However, death changed his plans in the middle of the day.

The house was awake, and everybody was moving about in their Saturday morning routines. I was in the kitchen, waiting not so patiently to see what Grandpa Robert had planned for his famous Saturday morning breakfast. As he put the bacon in the skillet, the sizzle was an unforgettable sound. This time, it would be for a different reason. As soon as he finished putting the bacon in the skillet, he turned to grab something out of the refrigerator and dropped to the floor, hard. I couldn't believe my eyes. As I stood there, waiting for him to try to get up or even cry for help, I realized he was motionless. He didn't make a sound.

I began screaming and ran to Mommie Dearest to tell her something was wrong with Grandpa Robert. When she came in and saw his lifeless body, she immediately called for help.

When the paramedics arrived, he had no pulse. He was gone. At that moment, I couldn't move. I just stood there in shock. Mommie Dearest hurried us into the bedroom, where we all just began to weep uncontrollably. *Who was going to love us now?*

In typical Mommie Dearest fashion, she didn't shed a tear, not one throughout the entire ordeal. She stood proud and tall, even as they carted her husband's dead body out of the house. She showed no emotion and didn't comfort us in any way.

We later learned that our ray of sunshine had passed away from a blood clot. It was a sudden death, and there was no suffering...on his part anyway. For us, it was a different story.

Javier and I still spent as much time together as we could. Even though we decided not to get married, he supported me during this time of bereavement. Shortly after my grandfather's death, he was offered a job in another city several hours away. When he accepted it, I felt abandoned and lost, even though he promised to return. To make matters worse, Mommie Dearest used the opportunity to drill in the *I told you so's*. She reminded me of how she told me this would happen and said Javier didn't want my "ugly, fat" self. Hearing "I told you so" a hundred times a day was quite depressing, and I struggled to make sense of it all.

The entire process scared me to death. I had no idea how it would all would work out. The pregnancy was extremely difficult, and I was growing more and more depressed. I spent a lot of time crying at the hands *and words* of Mommie Dearest. After Grandpa Robert's death, she added to her round of insults that I was the one who killed my grandpa by getting knocked up. She said his heart couldn't take the disappointment I had caused. Out of everything she said, that was the worst one yet. *How could a death like that be a child's fault?*

Secrets Never Stay Buried

During this challenging time, I turned to a remarkable woman that loved me dearly, my aunt, Fanny. She displayed the type of unconditional love I so desperately craved and needed.

One day, I went to visit her in tears. I finally told her all the things Mommie Dearest had been doing and saying. It just flowed out of me like a river. The things she had said in the past, the things she said that day, it all just came out. When I told her that Mommie Dearest said it was my fault that my grandpa was dead, she quickly informed me in a matter-of-fact way that it was all a lie. Everything. She was angry at the fact that Mommie Dearest would do that to her own pregnant grandchild. She pulled me close and assured me that his death was not my fault, reminding me that he was happy about the baby and was looking forward to the birth the following month.

Aunt Fanny then shared family secrets my siblings and I were never supposed to know. She began by telling me that Mommie Dearest was in love with a married man. She said he lived in a different city with his wife and children. The two had met early on in life and kept in contact over the years. One day, he contacted her to say that he would be in town and asked if they could get together for old times' sake. She agreed, and from that day on, the love affair began.

She knew he was married, but there was something about this man that Mommie Dearest couldn't disconnect from. She loved him more than life itself and desperately wanted a child with him. She figured if she couldn't have all of him, at least she could have a piece, her own little makeshift family. Mommie Dearest had two miscarriages before their daughter was born. This would be her only child, my mother, whom she adored because she was a part of the man she loved more than anything. The only man she had ever loved was a man she could never have.

Hearing this brought a new reality concerning our "perfect" grandmother. It seemed that she wasn't perfect at all. She was a hypocrite. Everything was a lie. I had spent so many years trying to earn Mommie Dearest's approval, hoping, in the end, I would be good enough to receive her love. But all this time, she was just as broken as me, if not more.

It explained so much: why she treated my grandpa the way she did and why she never approved of my relationship with Javier. I loved a man who didn't belong to anyone else, who seemed to care about me and wanted to be with me. Truth be told, she was the biggest reason he was not around because it crushed him to see how she treated me. One might even think she was jealous of my love story and did all she could to destroy it, and it almost worked.

Just then, things became very clear. When it came to Grandpa Robert, Mommie Dearest was never interested in love, only security. Money was her driving force. He was a hardworking man and did all he could to keep her happy, but she was never satisfied with him or with us. At that moment, I lost the little respect I had for Mommie Dearest.

Life Would Never Be the Same

Seventeen and pregnant, I was quickly approaching my due date and my high school graduation. Though I was about 110 pounds soaking wet, my belly was getting bigger and bigger. I was anxiously awaiting the arrival of the baby I felt moving inside of me.

Javier had moved back and frequently stopped by to pick me up. His mother had arranged for prenatal care with her doctor to ensure I had proper care during my pregnancy, and he was an excellent doctor. I had no idea what to expect when giving birth and only saw my mother go away and come back with a new baby each time. So to say I was naïve was an understatement. The doctor described, in detail, everything I needed to know about having a baby. He told me what to expect and explained when to go to the hospital for the big event. This information was helpful and scary all at the same time.

During my last few weeks of pregnancy, I continued my education at home and worked to prepare meals for Mommie Dearest's catering business. This task grew more and more difficult as time went on.

About two weeks before my due date, my family and I went shopping on what would turn out to be an eventful day. That morning, I woke up with a bit of a stomach ache but didn't think much of it. While we were out, I had a few slices of pizza, which made my stomach hurt even more. I thought I had overate and figured I would feel better once we got home.

Hours later, the stomach ache continued, and then all of a sudden, I had a strong urge to use the bathroom. I attempted to make it, only to realize I couldn't. A gush of fluid came running down my legs. Mommie Dearest heard the commotion and hurriedly got up. She then took one look at me and said it was time.

Because of the distance to the hospital, Mommie Dearest called an ambulance to pick me up and take me to the hospital. Mommie Dearest and my siblings followed behind us in her car. At this point, the pains were getting stronger, coming about every ten minutes and easing less and less. The ambulance ride to the hospital took about thirty minutes, but it felt like thirty hours.

When I arrived at the hospital, they took me back to a small room and checked me. They said I was ready and prepared for me to have the baby. The nurse called the doctor, and when he arrived, he told me to push several times, but the baby was not coming. The doctor quickly realized something was wrong when he saw the baby's foot instead of the head. The baby was breech.

He grabbed the forceps and attempted to turn the baby, but he was unsuccessful. This baby was going to make a grand entrance foot first. Several hours later, my daughter, Baby Abigail, was born in the middle of the night.

The first time I laid eyes on her, I knew my life would never be the same. Now I had someone that was a part of me and who would always love me. I would never feel alone again. She was the most beautiful baby I had ever laid eyes on, and of course, she looked more like Javier than me, making it a huge benefit.

Due to the challenging nature of the birth, I was in excruciating pain and was prescribed some pain medication, which put me to sleep for several hours. I'm not sure how long I was asleep, but my doctor soon woke me up, telling me that they noticed I had severe vaginal damage from the birth and the use of forceps. He said he would need to perform surgery to repair it.

I was put to sleep shortly after the conversation, and the procedure was performed. While I was asleep, a tube was placed in my throat, and during that process, my vocal cords were permanently damaged. After surgery, my singing voice was gone. I was no longer a soft soprano but an automatic alto. This was a huge disappointment, but no one seemed to care but me. I mean I was alive with my whole life ahead of me and a baby to call my own. We were both healthy. *What else mattered?*

Things Were Looking Up

After a few days in the hospital, I was discharged to go home. I faced some difficult days ahead as I healed from childbirth and surgery. Little tasks like changing diapers and feeding Baby Abigail were excruciating, but I kept pushing forward. Javier visited often and brought diapers and formula. He stayed for hours to spend time with me and get to know his beautiful baby girl. I was thrilled that things were finally looking up!

Ironically, Mommie Dearest drastically changed her attitude the first time she laid eyes on Abigail, and her heart was softened like we had never experienced before. She even offered to raise Abigail so I could go to college and make something of myself, to which I quickly responded, "No, thank you."

My sisters also stepped in to help me with taking care of Abigail. In fact, somewhere along the way, Janice decided Abigail was going to be her baby. She bought her clothes and dressed her up every day -- well, more like four or five times a day as if Abigail was her new little doll.

During this time, I was also able to complete my classes, although I struggled with whether I would accept my diploma in the mail or receive it during the graduation ceremony. I battled many negative thoughts. *I was seventeen years old with a child. What would all my classmates think about me? Should I be embarrassed to walk across that stage with a baby in the audience?*

Ultimately, I decided that I had earned the right to accept my diploma, and I was going to walk out there with my head held high. I qualified as a high school graduate, which was a great accomplishment considering everything I had been through. It was my life, and I could no longer worry about what people had to say. I was going to get what belonged to me, and that is precisely what I did. Still very sore from childbirth, I slowly walked across the stage, but I walked. And that moment sparked a fire within me. From that day forward, I promised myself that I would always fight for what I wanted and deserved.

A New Beginning

As planned, I moved out of Mommie Dearest's home the night of graduation. I asked my aunt and uncle if I could move in with them, and they said yes. I finally had a new beginning, one I would select for myself. I had achieved my goal and was finally out of Mommie Dearest's house.

Since Janice was taking such good care of Abigail, I agreed to let her remain there for a little while longer so I could get a job and work things out. This was my first shot at independence, and I wanted to give it my all. I knew Abigail was in good hands with my sisters, especially Janice, and I knew Mommie Dearest would not lay a hand on her. It seemed the pattern of favoring the firstborn daughter had continued. Mommie Dearest cherished Baby Abigail just as she had with my mother and her firstborn daughter, Janice.

Abigail was the first baby born in the family in fifteen years, and she brought a joy and happiness that had not been in that house for a long time. Mommie Dearest's heart was genuinely changed while Abigail was around, and it was apparent that she loved her.

Going to the Chapel and...

After moving out, I quickly found a job and began to save my money. I also visited Abigail often. Several months later, Javier approached me and said he wanted to talk. He told me he felt it was time for us to become a family, and I agreed. So, Javier and I decided to take the next big step and get married.

I wanted the fairy tale life: a wedding, a reception, and all the bells and whistles. However, Javier disagreed. We were young and fresh out of high school with a new baby. That was far from a fairy tale. So we planned to go to the courthouse and let the Justice of the Peace marry us. We decided to get our license and told everyone we would get married two days before Christmas. However, things didn't quite go as planned.

The courthouse was closed for Christmas that entire week, which meant we couldn't get the license or get married. So, being young and inexperienced, we pretended to be married when we visited our families during the holidays. It was hard pulling that off and included some stretching of the truth. Almost everyone believed us except for one family member, but Javier took care of that little distraction. Still, we knew we had to come up with a plan to actually get married.

After the holidays, we decided to take off work and get married. Javier worked out the details, so we were able to have our ceremony in a relative's living room. It was a small wedding with only an officiant, two witnesses, and me and Javier.

We also wanted to have a little honeymoon to celebrate. However, we both had to go to work the following Monday, so we knew we couldn't go far. Knowing how important this was to me, Javier came up with a plan for us to stay at our Aunt Fanny's after the wedding. We enjoyed our time, but we did not consummate our marriage because we wanted to respect Aunt Fanny's house. We were just happy to be married and together on our wedding night.

A Place Called Home

Prior to getting married, Javier and I had been looking for a place to live. A couple of weeks into our search, we found a little place we could call home. However, it was not immediately ready for us to move in. Although we spent the weekend together during our mini honeymoon, we had to return to living in separate homes for a few more weeks.

Once our home was ready, Javier and I decided to move in alone and get settled in before bringing Abigail home. Our house was just minutes away from Mommie Dearest's neighborhood, so we were still able to see Abigail almost every day. After a bit more honeymoon time, we both agreed it was time to bring our baby home.

I contacted Janice to let her know I would be coming to get Abigail as we were ready to settle in as a family, but she protested and insisted on keeping Abigail, saying she was just fine where she was. This fight went on and on, but I would not budge. I wanted my new family to be whole. Things between us were unpleasant for quite a while, but I eventually agreed to allow Janice to take Abigail a few days out of the week, although she would permanently live with me.

The transition into full-time motherhood was very difficult. Abigail did not want to sleep in her own bed, let alone her own room. Over the first year, getting her out of our bed and off the bottle proved to be two of the hardest things I had to do in my new role. I loved Abigail very much, but I didn't feel like I was good at this "mother" thing. *What did I know about parenting anyway?* Obviously, not much at all.

As time went on, Javier was offered a position that required us to relocate. We packed up and moved to an area where I didn't know anyone. I had no friends or family to lean on in my new role as a stay-at-home mother. So, it took a lot of improvising to make it work. I did my best to turn our house into a home for my new little family.

I soon began adjusting to my new life. It started out better than I could have imagined. I spent my days cooking for my new husband, caring for our daughter, and keeping up our tiny apartment. Music filled the house as I went through my daily routine, and I sang as loud as I wanted to with my newly changed voice. Javier worked very long hours, but some days, he would stop by for lunch to check on us. On several occasions, he went straight for dessert and left without eating. Those were some great memories.

Section III

FANTASY VS. REALITY

For Better
or Worse

As the months rolled by and the newness of being a young family began to wear off, Javier became restless. He began to stay out later and later on the weekends, spending more time with his friends than with his family. I spent most days alone, and when I asked him if he could spend more time at home, he complained that I was nagging him. The more I asked him to stay, the later he stayed out.

I soon learned I was pregnant again, and I was distraught. I didn't feel it was feasible to bring another child into a family that was going in the wrong direction. I explored all my options and decided I would not have the child.

Javier was not a lot of help because he had become self-absorbed and clueless about his family. Everything was all about him. He was caught in the grip of selfish, self-centered behavior, and I only became important when he wanted what got me in this situation in the first place, intimacy. In an attempt to be a good wife, I always responded in his favor. However, no matter how hard I tried, nothing could convince Javier to become a family man.

At the time, my problem-solving skills were mediocre at best. At that point, my husband was only coming home from work two or three days out of the week, and I felt hopeless to fix it. Feeling alone and afraid, I decided to travel five hours away to get an abortion. I wondered if this was how my mother felt when she made the decision to go alone.

I rode the bus to the appointment and tearfully began the process to end the pregnancy. I met with the nurse and answered some questions. However, as I mentally prepared to go through with the procedure, I was told that they couldn't continue and that I needed to leave. Without any explanation, it was canceled at the last minute.

Confused and overwhelmed, I began the long ride home. I cried for hours. All I could think about was how terrible my life would be having to take care of two children by myself. It seemed that Mommie Dearest was right. I had the chance to attend college and build a good life for myself and my child. She said if it was really love, it could have survived two years of college, but I would never know. Instead, I chose him. I was not trying to hear what anyone had to say, especially Mommie Dearest. I truly believed love would conquer all.

Staying Busy

I returned home late that evening and told Javier we needed to talk. I explained that things had to change. I told him what happened when I tried to have the abortion and explained that I could not raise two children alone. He said he understood and promised to do better.

Soon after that talk, I decided I needed to get out of the house. So, I began searching for a job. Javier did not want me to work, but because he was gone so much, I did the only thing I knew to do – stay busy.

Eventually, I got a job as a waitress, and I loved it. I could have adult conversations and truly enjoyed making people happy. I earned excellent tips and found a new family in my coworkers.

My favorite coworker was an older lady nicknamed "The Chef." She was a good listener and cared for me while I was at work. She made sure I ate every day since I was five months pregnant when I started the job.

More Secrets

Shortly after this promise, I was blindsided. Javier had been keeping secrets. One morning, I went into his billfold to get some money, and a picture of a baby fell out. This child seemed to be about a year old, and on the back of this picture was a note that read, "To my father." *What the hell!*

I had heard rumors of him having a child with another woman, but he continued to deny it. This was clearly proof that not only did he have a child, but he had been in contact with the child's mother. I immediately confronted him, and he had the nerve to respond by saying if I looked for trouble, I would find it. He said I had no business in his billfold and never explained or accepted responsibility that he lied and told me that was not his child.

News flash! This was the last straw. "I'm outta here!"

Prior to my departure, I broke every dish I could reach. I hit Javier with anything I could find, including the telephone, which he snatched from me and told me I wasn't going anywhere. I said okay, but as soon as he went to work the next morning, Abigail and I left.

Even in a new city, I was very resourceful. When I made up my mind to do something, I found a way. I took Abigail to spend a few days with my sisters at Mommie Dearest's but did not tell her what happened between Javier and me. The last thing I wanted to hear was "I told you so" from Mommie Dearest.

I then contacted Cousin Agnes and asked if I could spend a few days with her. She agreed, picked me up, and took me to her house. I was humiliated, to say the least. I was seven months pregnant with my second child and had to take a leave from my job. With no money, no transportation, and no husband, I had nothing.

Honor Thy Husband

After several weeks with Cousin Agnes, she sat me down and explained that I should return home to my husband. She said I needed to forgive him for lying and pointed out that the entire situation happened before the marriage. She told me that I should honor my vows.

Because I had a lot of respect for my cousin, I took her advice, and Abigail and I returned home. A few weeks later, our son, Jamal, was born. Eighteen months later, our third child was born, a girl whom we named Lachelle. We were having children so fast that it was difficult to focus on our marriage. Javier was becoming increasingly restless and said he was beginning to feel smothered. So he decided he needed some space and moved out.

I was devastated. When we married, we only had one child. Three years later, we had three children, and Javier was gone again. *What was I going to do alone with three children and a minimum-wage job?*

Of course, everything Mommie Dearest told me came flooding back. I remembered every time she told me I would never be anything and how ugly and stupid I was. I was completely overwhelmed by the situation. It was another failure. Something else I couldn't do right.

I began to cry uncontrollably, feeling nervous, hurt, and scared, wondering, *How I could do this by myself. I could not fathom doing this alone. I was still a child myself. How was I supposed to take care of three children? How will I survive?*

I returned to work, still heartbroken and unsure about the future. While waiting tables, I met a lady who worked for a well-to-do company. She noticed I was friendly and a hard worker and said she would put in a good word for me at her firm. I finally had a chance to do better. I was happy and sad all at the same time. Although I wasn't sure how it would all work out, it did.

Living Single

Eventually, Javier came home, and shortly after that, I was pregnant again. My third child was not even two years old; *how could I handle a fourth?* After careful thought, I decided I would not keep this baby, not this time. I did what I thought was best at the time and tried to move on. I was struggling, my marriage was struggling, and I desperately wanted to believe it would all work out. However, Javier soon left again, and this time, he stayed gone for almost a year. I knew where he was and asked him to come home several times. Yet, my attempts failed miserably.

In an attempt to move on, I worked lots of hours and was able to make ends meet. I also got involved with a man, which proved to be a huge mistake. I thought my marriage was over and got caught up in believing he cared about me. In reality, it was all about what he wanted from me.

Although I ended the relationship quickly, I did have some fun in the process. One night, he took me to a little place in the country, and we danced like I had never danced before. Just like my mother, I loved to dance, and I was pretty good at it, but Javier didn't do things like go out dancing. Although that experience was negative, I was able to walk away with some good memories.

Javier must have had an inkling that I was moving on because he started coming around again, and eventually, we reconciled. To put it mildly, we had a rocky relationship, but I was doing all I knew to keep it together. We were a young couple that started out as friends. Yet, early in the marriage, we began to grow apart and didn't realize what the problem was. We had no idea how to repair a young love gone wrong.

Surprise, Surprise

A couple of years had gone by when I started to feel some extreme stomach pain. I brushed it off for a day or two but finally decided to see the doctor. He ran all kinds of tests, and when the results came back, to my surprise, I was pregnant. And not just a little pregnant. According to the lab, I was about six months. I couldn't believe it. *Six months pregnant!* I hadn't had any of the symptoms I had during other pregnancies, and I did not gain any weight.

A week or so after the doctor's visit, it seemed like someone put a basketball under my blouse. I blew up almost overnight. Sure enough, three months later, my last child was born.

Six weeks later, I attempted to return to work. I had a good job that I truly enjoyed, but we soon realized that day care was going to consume my entire check. So, Javier and I agreed that I would work nights and he would work days. Unfortunately, he did not keep his end of the bargain. His addiction was becoming a problem, and he kept getting into trouble. At times, he was too impaired to drive, and his irresponsibility forced me to have to leave work to go get the children. Because this happened multiple times, I eventually lost my job due to violation of the attendance policy.

Although we had beautiful children, I didn't want to have any more. So, I spoke with my doctor and decided to have a tubal ligation. The doctor required Javier's signature, but he did not want to sign. He felt I was too young to get my tubes tied. I not so politely reminded him that I was the one giving birth to these children and said if he wanted to live to see another day, he would sign the papers immediately. He hesitantly signed.

Everything Happens for a Reason

This was not the first time I wanted to get my tubes tied. After my third child was born, I requested to get my tubes tied, but the doctor refused to perform the procedure because I had been in a horrible accident just weeks before.

On my way to work one morning, a truck pulled beside me and decided to change lanes. I must have been in his blind spot because he did not see me. Driving extremely fast, he ran me off the road and head-on into a light pole. I was six months pregnant at the time, and the steering wheel had coupled around my stomach. In excruciating pain, I was rushed to the hospital, where I stayed until our baby was born two weeks later. At just four pounds, he was a tiny premature baby. He struggled to breathe because his lungs were not strong enough. It was touch and go for a while, but he was able to leave the hospital six weeks later.

After being denied the surgery the first time, I tried every type of birth control on the market, but nothing worked. My aunt would tell me, "You a hot little mama, just like yo' mama." I guess she was right. But I believe everything happens for a reason, even when you don't understand what those reasons are.

Sharing is...

As time went on, things continued to fall part. His addiction to alcohol was beginning to affect our marriage and his relationship with our children. During this time, a friend of mine reached out and asked if she could live with us until she could get on her feet. I talked it over with Javier, and he agreed. I thought this would be a breath of fresh air. We had been friends for a long time, and we shared everything. She knew all of my secrets, and I knew hers.

She was also a big help with the children while I was at work. Since I couldn't count on Javier, she stepped in and began babysitting them after school. She would help them with their homework, cook dinner, and get them ready for bed. I was so grateful to have a helping hand when I needed it most.

Unfortunately, she took our relationship for granted and began sharing more than secrets with me. I thought it was implied that we could not share my husband, but she did not get the memo. As my woman's intuition kicked in, I began to notice the atmosphere in my house was different, and it seemed more and more uncomfortable when she was around. When I began hearing rumors that they were having an affair, it confirmed what I was already sensing inside. I had had enough!

Gracefully Broken

Against all rational, I went to see Mommie Dearest of all people. When I told her what was happening in my marriage, she said, "I told you that boy was no good years ago, but you wouldn't listen. You need to divorce him and admit you were wrong for not listening to me." Of course, that was the last thing I wanted to hear.

I returned home to an empty apartment. Feeling alone with no viable solution at the time, I convinced myself I was a failure. It seemed Mommie Dearest was right when she said I was ugly, I'd never be nothing, and nobody would ever want me. I convinced myself to do my babies and the world a favor and just give up. Life was more than I could handle. So, I decided to end it.

As with my character, I planned it out. I stayed up all night looking for the insurance policies and tried to figure out the best way to ensure my babies would be taken care of if I was out of the picture and Javier remained selfish and self-centered.

After a few days of no sleep or food, I decided to kill myself and make it look like an accident. I changed the beneficiary on the policies to ensure someone I trusted would be the guardian of my children and ensure they were financially taken care of.

I thought I was as prepared as one could be in this situation. I had covered all the bases. Insurance policy, check. Accident scene, check. Medication to prevent pain, check. And, of course, some good music, check. I knew it wouldn't be easy, but it was time to follow through.

The next morning, I went to my children and gave them all a big goodbye hug and took special care to explain to them how much I love them. I said, "Mama is going through a little bit of a tough time right now, but we'll be together real soon." Abigail immediately knew something wasn't right, but I intentionally avoided all of her questions. She was such a smart young lady with an old soul, and she knew me very well.

I had devised a plan to mix my meds right there in the bedroom so Javier could find me and tell people it must have been an accident because I had been a little stressed lately. However, my plan was foiled because he didn't return for days, and when he returned, we entered the same cycle we had done so many times before.

Javier had a way with words. Whenever we had an altercation, he would stay gone for days and then come home and make it seem like it was all my fault. His reverse psychology seemed to work every time. This time, we can call it divine intervention because I was so glad to see him that I momentarily forgot about the issues we had prior to his leaving.

The joy didn't last very long. A few days later, he would leave again. I knew I needed some time to figure things out. So, I asked a friend if the children could stay with her. She agreed, and I returned home, finding myself alone once again.

During this time, I spent my days sitting in the middle of the floor, listening to *Do You Still Love Me?* by *Meli'sa Morgan* on repeat. My home was no longer bright, cheery, and organized but dark and in shambles. There was almost a calming effect to the darkness. I had lost my zeal for life.

I decided to follow through with my original plan and take the meds. I figured he would have to come back sooner or later, but as I attempted to execute the plan, I couldn't seem to get the look of my children's faces out of my mind. Even though I was emotionally, mentally, and psychologically messed up, the love for those babies hindered my plan.

When I finally got up the nerve to see it through, my plan was thwarted again. An uninvited visitor stopped by to check on me. After knocking for over 30 minutes, she tried the door handle and realized the door was open. She immediately knew something was wrong because my door was always locked.

As she slowly walked in, she was shocked to see my house in such disarray. She walked over to where I was sitting and began calling my name over and over again, but I did not reply. I could not reply. I felt as if I was no longer there. She then helped me up and took me straight to the emergency room for help.

That evening, it was determined that I had suffered a nervous breakdown. I had finally broke. The wreckage of my life came tumbling down on me all at once. I couldn't seem to find one reason to hold on, one reason to live.

I was admitted to the hospital and remained there for three weeks. During that time, I was encouraged to face my past. The beatings. My mother's death. My failing marriage. All of it. I had to dig deep to identify the reason why I no longer had the desire to live. My treatment included putting me in a hypnotic state daily, and I spent 21 days begging my grandmother to stop beating me. During each session, I reverted back to that little girl who tried to convince my grandmother that I was a good girl.

One of the women that worked at the hospital saw something in me. She would stop by to care for me daily, and she was so encouraging. Although she never said anything about God, her actions were kind and intentional. Interestingly enough, I would come across her again years later when I learned that God had a plan all along.

In receiving the care I needed, I soon realized my relationship with Javier was not good for me or the children. I knew I had a choice to make: Javier or the children. Of course, I chose the children.

The Fairy Tale Ends

Our off-and-on, rocky relationship had lasted twelve years by the time I finally had enough. After being discharged from the hospital, I decided to divorce Javier. To him, it seemed that anywhere was better than being home, so I figured I would let him be free. However, there was one problem: I couldn't afford a divorce.

After some searching, I was able to find a program that assisted low-income individuals with legal services and signed up to begin the process. Javier refused to agree to the divorce and genuinely believed if he didn't show up to court, the divorce couldn't happen. However, he was sorely mistaken. It took nine long months, but it did happen without him.

For the first time, I was the one who wanted him to leave, yet he refused to go. Javier stayed for months, refusing to believe the divorce was final. He was finally convinced when the automatic payments for child support began. Javier was fuming and blamed me, but I couldn't understand why he was so mad. I had been trying to tell him for months, but he was not interested in hearing about the divorce. A few weeks later, he moved out.

Me Time

Because Javier couldn't decide whether he wanted to be single or married, I did my best to focus on myself. I decided it was time for a new beginning, and the first step was to get out of that apartment. Although there were some memories, the bad was more prevalent. I had to move.

I searched for apartments within the same school district so the children could stay in the same schools. However, the only place that would rent to me was in a different school district. The children were disappointed, but they understood the situation.

While working full-time at a fast-food restaurant during the day, I decided to take a computer course at night that would help me qualify for a well-paying job that could better prepare me to care for my children. I also made the difficult decision to reach out to Mommie Dearest and ask for help. At the time, I had no one else to go to. She agreed to assist only if Javier remained out of the picture. I desperately needed assistance with rent while in school since I couldn't work a second job, so I agreed to her terms.

Javier eventually found out where the children and I were living and started coming by. At first, he would come by while I was away. However, as his visits became more frequent, I started seeing him more often. He knew it was hard for me to resist that thing that we had between us. He was a charming man, and even though I had initiated the divorce, I still loved him and missed him very much. I knew I shouldn't have taken him back, but the heart doesn't always make good choices.

Javier didn't move in but was visiting quite often. One random night, when he stopped by, I allowed him to spend the night. Ironically, Janice stopped by as well. When Javier answered the door, he was shirtless. Janice ran straight to Mommie Dearest and told her Javier was back and that we were living together. Although that was not entirely true, Mommie Dearest was MAD. The financial assistance she provided immediately stopped, and she refused to help from that point on. The deal was that there would be no Javier, and I didn't hold up my end of the bargain. Once again, I had disappointed Mommie Dearest.

With one month of school left, I just couldn't allow myself to quit. I did my best to push through and was able to complete my courses. The faculty was so impressed with my story, they gave me an award at the ceremony for extraordinary perseverance.

Javier, Mommie Dearest, and my children all came to my graduation, and when I was presented with the award, the Dean shared my story. He explained that although I was newly divorced with four children and working full time, I still made sure to devote time and energy to my studies. Because of my drive and dedication, I had never missed a class and maintained a 4.0 GPA. It was a great accomplishment.

For the second time in my life, I achieved my goal and proved that hard work does pay off. I thought maybe that would be the night that Mommie Dearest would finally admit that she was proud of me, but that didn't happen. Instead, she told me I would have never been able to accomplish that feat without her. Once again, I was disappointed. I still had not received the long-awaited recognition I longed for from Mommie Dearest.

The Struggle is Real

After graduation, I secured a decent-paying job and began trying to start my new life. However, no matter how hard I tried, there was just not enough money coming in. My schedule constantly rotated, and I often had to work nights. It was not the best life for me and my children. Plus, I was hired for all the wrong reasons. I was a token because of my race and sex and filled a quota.

With no financial help, the rent and the bills continued to fall behind. At the time, Javier was not able to help us because he was caught up in a world of addiction that left him unable to take care of himself. So I did what I had to and moved in with my Aunt Fanny, who always had an open door for me and my babies. No questions asked! This was a win-win for me. My aunt was always home, so it solved the problem of working nights and allowed me to catch up financially.

After the one-year probationary period, I was terminated from my job. They decided I was not a good fit yet gave no feedback regarding why. I figured there was no need to linger or focus on what I couldn't change. Since I had saved some money, I decided to take a break and spend time with my children. I moved out of my aunt's house and, once again, got my own place.

Javier did not move with us, and I purposely did not let him know where we lived. Unfortunately, the children had to change schools again, but this time they were happy. They returned to the school they previously attended and reconnected with their friends, which was good for everyone.

My previous job had been very stressful, and I worked a lot of overtime, which proved difficult for me and my children. That was the only period during my children's lives that I had missed birthdays and holidays. Work had become the priority. So I spent the next six months trying to make up for it. When they came home from school, I had dinner on the table, and we celebrated birthdays in style. We had a great time and enjoyed the opportunity to focus on each other.

Once the money started getting low, I decided it was time to find another job that was about twenty minutes away. It was a bit far, but I took it because the money was getting low. The pay was decent, and my work schedule was much better for the family. However, because the rent was still fairly high, we had to move again. I was able to find an apartment not far from our current apartment, which meant that the children could stay in the same schools.

By this time, Javier had taken a job out of town, and we were not on speaking terms. Whenever he called to speak to the children, I would make myself scarce because hearing his voice brought back all the feelings I wanted to forget. I still loved him dearly, but I did not love what he was doing or the fact that his family was not a priority.

Looking for Love in All the Wrong Places

The children and I found a routine, and we were finally getting on the right track. I even tried a couple of relationships, which failed miserably. At the time, I didn't understand that my heart needed to heal first. I continuously compared each man to Javier, and no one seemed to be able to measure up.

One man I was dating came close, and I figured it was time to settle for some stability. After all, Mommie Dearest settled, and she and Grandpa Robert made it work. So, I considered marrying him as a way of moving on. He really was not all that, but he treated me kindly.

One day, Abigail overheard him telling someone, "I'm not going to marry that chick for real." When asked why, he answered, "I can give you four reasons." When I confronted him, he admitted he said it but said he "didn't mean it the way it came out." Yeah right! That was the end of that.

After ending that relationship, I met another gentleman. We began dating, and he was wonderful. He treated me and my children like they were his responsibility. He was kind, respectful, giving, and loving, but there was just one problem: He was not Javier. I truly wanted to love him, but it wasn't fair to pretend. Eventually, I told him I was still in love with Javier, and we ended our relationship.

I gave dating one final try, and it turned out to be a disaster. Even though we were divorced and Javier was living his life, he made it his business to be sure no man got too close to "his woman."

After a while, I decided I would give up on dating. I started to question this whole "love" thing. *What if I was never meant to be loved? Or was I looking for love in all the wrong places?* Either way, it was tiresome, and I didn't want to do it any longer.

After my dating days, I was spending most of my downtime at home when a friend invited me to go dancing. I loved to dance and had a great time. So, I started going regularly, and Javier knew this. He would pop up from time to time and ask me to dance. Of course, I couldn't resist.

One night he invited me to his place so we could talk. He said he wanted to do better by our children, but I knew better. He didn't want to talk about our children at 2 o'clock in the morning. I knew what the plan was, and I totally gave in. Once I was reminded of what I had been missing, the emotions came flooding back. We started getting together secretly more and more often, but when he stopped by to see the children, we would pretend we were co-parenting. Eventually, that would all change.

One Foot In

One night, I wanted to go out and needed a trustworthy babysitter. Since I didn't have any relatives living nearby, I asked one of Javier's family members, Anita, to watch them. She agreed, but only if I agreed to go to church and pick up the children from there. I said I would but had no intentions of going to church. When I arrived to pick them up after service,

Anita told me she wouldn't keep them anymore unless I went to church and actually stayed for the service.

I finally gave in and went to church with her. Abigail was excited and enjoyed the service. She asked if we could go back and said she wanted to join. The next time they stayed with Anita, we went to church with her again. That day, I was touched by the Word of God, and my heart was pricked to give my life to Christ. I was very shy and didn't want to walk down the aisle, but I was sure that was the day I needed to give my heart to Christ. What a glorious winter day that was, and I felt different in a weird kind of way. At the time, I didn't truly understand the fullness of what I had just committed to. I knew I needed a change in my life because things were not working. *So, what did I have to lose?*

I had previously attended church and vacation bible school and even sung in church choirs, but I never really connected with God in a way that made a difference. In fact, while growing up, attending church was just something to do to get out of the house. It was a plus for me because I loved to sing, and the church had plenty of opportunities for that. Yet, somehow, some way, this day was different.

I started taking my children to church regularly but continued doing the same things. In fact, when I went out to dance, I saw a few church people there as well. In my mind, it must have been okay to go out as long as I went to church on Sundays. However, I would soon find out that was not necessarily the case. Time would prove differently.

The thing about going to church before you completely surrender to Christ is it has the potential to become mediocre. It was becoming something else to do as if to say, "Okay, God. I showed up today." I didn't have much to give, but I left it as, *God, you know my heart.*

As I continued attending church, I met friends I would get to know outside of church. I also got mixed up in some activities that I will regret for the rest of my life. At the time, I would get love from wherever I could find it. At one point, I encountered two people in my family (who will remain unnamed) that wanted to love me and my children in a sick kind of way. I seemed to be meat for the taking. I was still young and inexperienced with people, relationships, and life in general, and not to mention living in a new city.

After several months with one foot in the door and the other on its way to hell, I found myself having a "thing" with a gentleman I had met. He said he was divorced and lived alone, so it wasn't an affair or even a relationship. It was just a "thing" that we did when we met up. Our "thing" was exciting to the extinct that the passion came from the thrill of not getting caught, but that didn't last long.

We were at his house during our last meeting when there was a knock at the door. The woman that used to live there, *according to him,* came looking for him. She barged in and started looking in rooms, under the beds, and in closets while screaming, "Where is that -----?!" This so-called single man started acting innocent and pretending like he didn't know what she was talking about. They continued to argue and swap profanity for over an hour until she finally left, slamming the door behind her.

I remained hidden in a closet, afraid to move, breathe, or speak. Sweating like crazy and scared to death, I thought about what would have happened if that door opened. *What would I do?*

I quickly realized this was not love, and it was no longer fun. It was time for me to get my life together. That day was my turning point.

Fairy Tales and Fantasies

At this point, Javier and I had been divorced for a couple of years, and I had made some significant changes in my life. One day, I got a call that Javier had gotten hurt. Apparently, he had been mugged when walking one evening and had a few broken ribs and lots of bruising. He needed a place to stay while he recovered, and I just couldn't say no. So I allowed him to come home. Although we did not sleep in the same bed and were not together, it sent mixed messages to the children. The boys always wanted their daddy around and were big advocates for him.

Because of our emotional and mental connection and the time spent together in a platonic relationship, the fire between us was reignited. Javier wanted to get back together and convinced me he was ready for his family to be whole again. It took a little time, but I eventually agreed but with one condition: I wanted a wedding this time.

Javier got on his feet and got a job, and we had a beautiful wedding. We were given so much favor that our $300 wedding looked like a $3,000 wedding. My dress, valued at $300, was discounted to $100 by the store owner after hearing my story, and my beautiful bouquet didn't reflect the fact that it was made from simple flowers from the 5 & Dime Store. Our friends and family came together to do whatever they could to make this day memorable for us, everyone except for Mommie Dearest. But I couldn't focus on her. My fairy tale was finally coming true!

My wedding day was awe-inspiring. When the doors to the sanctuary opened up, I stood there speechless with my eldest son, Jamal, by my side. The church was decorated exquisitely in ivory with hot pink accents. Ivory drapes lined the aisle, and flowers were on every other bench. Javier was standing at the altar under an arch made of flowers, waiting with a look of pure joy as I walked down the aisle. Tears welled in my eyes as I slowly made my way to him. After all we had been through, we were once again dedicating our lives to each other. He looked at me as if I was the most beautiful woman in the world, and for the first time in my life, I believed it.

Back to the Real World

Our first year being remarried was worse than all the years we had been married before. Javier had started drinking and was making dumb decisions. He was literally being controlled by the spirits he was drinking. I couldn't understand why he said he wanted his family back if he wasn't going to do right by us. We were getting older, and so were the children.

For our son Antwone's twelfth birthday, Javier promised to take him to the amusement park, which was an hour's drive away. Antwone was so excited he got up with the sun and got dressed. My baby sat on his knees on the couch, looking out the window, waiting for his daddy until he fell asleep later that night. Javier never came home.

That did it. I couldn't take it anymore. I moved everything out of that house that day, leaving only the sofa and a television for Javier. That was the day he decided he would get some help.

Javier was gone to rehab for about a month, but I was not sure if I wanted to reconcile this time around. I had been embarrassed and humiliated by what he was doing outside our home because he was no longer hiding his extracurricular activities. Everything was made public. It's easy to turn a blind eye when no one knows what is going on, but when everyone knows, it brings a new light to the situation. I was being betrayed all over again. The deceit was no longer hidden. It seemed it had no end, and finding out about the child, being constantly lied to, and his drinking was just too much for me to bear.

When Javier decided to do what he did, I couldn't understand why God would allow this. *If He was real, why would He let Javier continue to treat me this way now that I am a changed woman? Don't I deserve better?* I was attending church regularly and learning a lot about Jesus and His love. Yet I still struggled with the reality I was living. So I did just as I had done with everything else: I kept myself busy. I went running in, willing to work wherever needed. However, I soon learned not everybody in the church building is there to serve the same Master. Evil is also present, doing everything possible to get you to switch teams.

I endured a lot of pain in the church building, and it would take years to understand that GOD is not confined to a building. When I accepted Jesus as my Savior and Lord, it took me a while to learn that He was with me no matter where I went. There was a lot of trial and error; some backsliding, sinning, and repentance and then more backsliding, sinning, and repentance before I understood that I was never alone.

I learned valuable lessons while serving in the ministry. One such lesson was that not everyone would like me, and not everyone would see my heart or take the time to get to know me before they judged me.

Around the time I joined the church, my eldest child, Abigail, was in the bathroom and overheard two women speaking ill of me. I only had two dresses to wear to church at the time, and I wore them every other Sunday. That was all I had as a single parent, barely making ends meet. One day, I read that Jesus said come as you are, so that was precisely what I did.

Abigail was a little firecracker, just like her grandmother, and she was ready to fight. With tears in her eyes, she came to me and told me what was said. I told her not to worry about them and that they didn't matter, but seeing the hurt on her face broke me down privately.

I continued to worship there for many years, but sadly enough, I felt rejected where I was supposed to feel welcomed and defeated where I was supposed to feel victorious. But God! He placed a special woman there, who, ironically enough, I met when I suffered a nervous breakdown before I decided to divorce Javier the first time.

Heaven-Sent

One Sunday morning, I decided to attend Sunday School, which was a thirty-minute class that started before morning worship. When the teacher stood up and began to pray, I thought I recognized her, but I couldn't remember where I knew her from, and she never reminded me. It would be years before I knew she was the same woman from the hospital who helped care for me.

As I began to learn more about Jesus, He began to reveal some things to me. I believe she was assigned as an angel to watch over me and guide me. She taught me how to understand the Word of God, she prayed for me until I could learn to pray for myself, and she encouraged me to ignore fools that talk about people in the church bathrooms. She tried to warn me that it was not good to socialize with everybody in the church building. The decision not to heed that warning would haunt me for years.

She was a gift placed in my life for over twenty-five years, and she loved me dearly. She taught me how to teach God's Word in a way a child could understand it, which led me to the thing I loved doing most.

After healing my heart, I was able to work with children for several years. I had the chance to see them blossom, grow, and go on to live productive, successful lives, and that was the gift that kept on giving. I cherished those days because it allowed me to fill that void of emptiness by pouring into children who were open, pure, and lovable.

Although I did not want to go through a nervous breakdown, it taught me a valuable life lesson: We can overcome anything if we are willing to keep fighting.

Patients Require Patience

After Javier dealt with his demons, he reminded me of that boy I had met and got to know in class so many years before. However, I still found it hard to trust him. He had broken every promise he had made to me, time and time again, and I struggled to get past it.

Over time, I began to notice the changes in his behavior. He was becoming a man of his word, not just talk, but action. And his change was changing me. I started to let my guard down and slowly began trusting him again.

After giving up drinking, Javier began to have some health problems that required quite a few surgeries on his knee. The problem was he was a horrible patient. It was difficult being his nurse since he didn't like being taken care of, but I stayed by his side every step of the way.

Throughout this season, Javier was unable to work. So, he decided to go to school to change occupations. He went through a course on business and got his degree. Afterward, he began working full-time as a self-employed entrepreneur. He went from working with his hands to working on contracts.

Our family was finally coming back together when death came knocking. Cousin Agnes, who had been so instrumental in my life, passed unexpectedly. This was such a significant blow since she was the person who I ran to when times were hard. She was full of great wisdom and advice.

Seven months later, Mommie Dearest became very ill. She was rushed to the hospital, where they ran some tests and discovered she had cancer. Because the cancer had spread all over her body, all they could do was keep her comfortable.

About a week later, Javier and I were on our way to church with the children when I received a phone call. It was Mommie Dearest calling from the hospital. She said she had fallen out of bed, and no one would help her get up. The hospital was a good hour away from where we lived, and it made no sense as to why she was calling me for help.

Javier and the children went to church, and I went to check on Mommie Dearest. When I arrived, she was in bed, and the nurses had no idea what I was talking about. I thought it could be the medication, but Janice had been in the room with her the entire time.

As I sat down, she told Janice she could leave and asked me to stay, which was puzzling. Looking back on our history, Janice was always the one she wanted by her side. Nevertheless, I did as she asked and ended up staying for weeks.

One evening, as I was on the cot trying to find a comfortable position, I noticed Mommie Dearest was wide awake, looking at me like she had something to say. She had an apologetic look on her face, but she didn't say a word. I finally said, "Go to sleep. You need your rest," to which she replied, "I'll pay you for staying with me." I ignored the statement, rolled over, and went back to sleep.

The following day, I got up without having had much rest. Mommie Dearest was already awake. I asked her if she wanted her bed changed, and she did. So I got her up and sat her in the chair. They brought breakfast, which was grits with butter, sugar, and bacon crumbled up in it. This was the first meal she had since I arrived that she actually enjoyed and finished.

She asked me to pray for her because her breath was short and she was in pain. As I started praying for her, I was led to ask her if she was saved. She looked right through me and didn't answer. So I went over the plan of salvation with her. She said she did believe in Jesus. She believed He was crucified, died, and rose with all power in heaven and earth, and she confessed her sins.

They put clean sheets on her bed, and I cleaned her up with a sponge bath. Once she was all freshened up, I said, "Now, get you some rest." She looked at me and said, "Okay. I am going to rest." She fell asleep shortly afterward.

While at the hospital, I went to the chapel to pray daily at 10:00 a.m. On this particular day, I had this strange feeling that I needed to call my siblings and tell them to come and tell Mommie Dearest goodbye if they wanted to do so while she was alive. They heeded my advice and came to the hospital. Each had their time with her and then left. Later that evening, she took her last breath. Mommie Dearest was gone.

What was surprising to me was, at that moment, I felt nothing. I wasn't sad. I didn't scream. There was nothing. Just shock that it happened so quickly. That was the first time I had ever witnessed someone take their last breath.

I called the nurse, and she confirmed the time of death. Then, I contacted the funeral home. It was up to me to ensure her wishes were honored. She had everything arranged and paid for, so all I had to do was type up the program.

The service for Mommie Dearest was different. I felt like I was in my fantasy world again, pretending it wasn't really happening. The gravity of the situation didn't hit me until three weeks later when I woke up at 3:00 a.m. and cried for hours. I later realized that not only was I mourning her death, I was also mourning the fact that she died without ever telling me she was proud of me or that I turned out to be a good person. She hadn't said anything to validate me and make me feel like I had finally earned her love.

One might say coming to the hospital was her way of validating me. However, I felt that was God's assignment. I still desired to hear those words directly from her.

In The Midst of the Storm

Not only was this a difficult time for us, we were under severe financial constraints. Javier's surgery was the same year that Mommie Dearest died, and during this time, I had to take a leave from work.

After Mommie Dearest passed, I returned to work. I was immediately called into my supervisor's office, and I thought for sure I was going to be fired. Instead, they informed me they were going to pay me for the entire time I was off tending to Mommie Dearest. This was a miracle since it had been months since either of us had received a paycheck. Javier was approved for disability three months later.

Who's My Daddy?

Mommie Dearest was gone, which meant I no longer had a maternal connection in any form. I felt like I didn't have a place of belonging and thought about my mother and the complicated situation with my father, or should I say "daddy." I still had so many questions, and this led me on a search that would continue to this very day. It started with the question, "Where is my father?" That apparently was a million-dollar question that, even today, I don't know the answer to.

During my mother and her husband's eight-year marriage, nine children were born. Five lived, and four died. However, as the secrets surfaced, it appeared that he was not MY father.

When I was about ten or eleven, a gentleman came to my grandmother's home and told me he wanted to take me to get some ice cream, and my grandmother agreed. What little girl doesn't want ice cream? So, I walked with him to the ice cream parlor down the street from where we lived.

As we sat and ate ice cream, he began talking in what sounded like riddles. I had no idea what he was talking about. My focus was on the ice cream and not on this strange man I had never seen before. I licked that ice cream like crazy, in awe of how it was melting faster than I could lick it.

He finally threw his ice cream away and just cut to the chase, saying, "I courted your mother around the time she became pregnant with you. I believe you are my daughter, and I want to do right by you." None of that made sense to me, and I had no idea what this man was talking about, and that started a spiral of confusion in my life that left me feeling empty in so many ways.

I learned many years later that he gave my grandmother this same spiel, and she saw it as a grand opportunity to cash in on some extra dollars. So, she rolled with it. He would come by and bring her $100 every now and then, and she, in turn, would let me visit him at his house, where he lived with his wife and their children.

The first time he took me on a visit, he introduced me as his daughter, and for the most part, they all accepted me. His wife was a precious woman. She always treated me as one of her own children and never said an unkind word to me or about me, *as far as I knew*. She supported her husband and saw me as a child caught up in the sins of two adults.

As the years passed, my siblings would make fun of me because I had "a new daddy." They would tell me I would have to leave Mommie Dearest's house and move in with him. As a little girl, I had no one to talk to about it, so I held it all in.

Whenever we would go to church with my aunt, he would show up and tell everyone I was his daughter. It was humiliating and embarrassing because I wanted to be like my siblings and share the same father. I didn't want all the theatrics of this newly learned fact.

A couple of years later, a lady from Colorado came by to visit and asked my grandmother if she could take me shopping because she wanted to talk to me about something. My grandmother said I could go, and we headed to the clothing store. The lady bought me a few outfits and then told me, "I think you are my niece. Your mother had a fling with my brother around the time she got pregnant with you, and you look just like his children." I thought, *Wow! So, I have another daddy?*

She then went on to say that no one could know, and this would be our little secret because if his wife found out, she would leave him. She promised to visit often so she could get to know me. This went on for a few years, and then she disappeared. However, she did send nice things every now and then, and my grandmother got a little money from her as well.

As I got older, into my pre-teen years, I was told there was another man who had a great love for alcohol that hung out with my mother a lot leading up to the time she became pregnant with me. The lady who relayed this information told me the other two men were not my father; he was. I knew the man she was speaking of and had seen him almost every day for years, yet he never mentioned a thing. She explained that he had known it all along but never had anything to offer me, so he kept quiet. He knew my grandmother would have nothing to do with him or let him have anything to do with me.

Finally, I had an opportunity to speak to him and ask him point blank, "Are you my father?" He said, "Yes, that's what your mother told me." I asked him why he never said anything, and he repeated what I had been told, "Because I had nothing to offer you." That saddened me greatly because he was the first man to say my mother told him I was his. However, we didn't speak of it again after that day.

I wondered, *Would it have made a difference if he had stepped up early in my life?* Was it possible the emptiness of not belonging or feeling whole would have disappeared had I heard those words earlier? Those questions would also go unanswered.

So, there we have it. Three different men claim to have been with my mother during the months prior to her conceiving me, and none of them are listed on my birth certificate. Searching for the answer to the question, "Who's my daddy," continued to leave me extremely confused.

As the plot thickens, I finally got the courage to discuss this topic with the man who was married to my mother at the time of her death and listed as my father on my birth certificate. I begged him, "Please tell me the truth. Are you my father or not?" He said, "Yes, I am your father. Your mother never told me any different."

Four men admitted to being my father, but not one rescued me from the hell I endured for most of my life. This left me with a complex about men, love, relationships, and faithfulness at a time when none of it made sense to my messed-up mind.

Over the years, I had been told to get over the fact that I did not know who my daddy was. "What difference does it make? You're grown now." Statements like that usually come from people who know who their parents are. Although I have two families that accepted me, no questions asked, I still wonder what life would have been like if I had known who my daddy was. Yet I've realized I can't control decisions I had nothing to do with.

My Father Figure

After years of searching for answers, I turned to my Spiritual Father for guidance. He had been in my life for over twenty years. Even when I moved away, he continued to treat me like I had never left and was always happy to see me. We visited often, and I got a chance to share with him how much I loved him and what a blessing he was in my life. I repeatedly reminded him that the seeds he sowed fell on good ground.

Although he passed, and I knew he won't suffer anymore, I selfishly wished he could still be here. He was the only father figure consistently in my life, filling the void I had longed for and needed for so many years.

He introduced me to Jesus the way I needed to be introduced, one scripture at a time, and he invested time and love. Although he was not my biological father nor blood relation, we were connected by the Blood of Jesus. He also taught me how to be the woman of God I am today.

He once taught a lesson that really stuck with me. He said if you want people to treat you right, show them by how you treat them. In another Bible Study lesson, he taught about love and asked the question, "How many of you have ever fallen in love?" Of course, many of us raised our hands, and he quickly told us to put our hands down. Then, he gently explained that "falling in love" was used as a process to be with someone. He said, "Truth is: We don't fall in love; we choose to love an individual."

I never forgot that lesson, and as I looked back over my life, I remembered how many times I chose to love, chose to forgive, and chose to forget. I realized I agreed with him wholeheartedly. I chose to love. It was my choice, and I could have changed my mind whenever I got ready to, but I didn't.

He taught me many life-changing lessons that made me take a look in the mirror at my choices and consider how my choices and decisions didn't always align with the Word of God. When I would talk to him about situations and circumstances in my life, his answer would always come from the Word of God, and he would finish our conversations with "Let's pray about it."

If I were to remember the one lesson that stood out the most, I would choose the lesson he taught me about tithing. Many people have opinions about tithing belonging in the Old Testament, but not Pastor. He believed the entire Bible was still true no matter what year it was, and if we obeyed it, God would bless us.

In my early years as a baby Christian, I went to Pastor with a problem. I only had enough money to pay either my tithes or my electric bill. At that time, I was divorced and raising four children. I told him, "If I don't pay the electric bill, it will be cut off on Tuesday morning. If I didn't pay my tithes, I would be disobeying God. So, what do I do?" He replied, "It's simple. Pay your tithes because God promised to supply your needs, and electricity is a need. If God doesn't come through for you, call me, and I will give you the money to pay your electric bill myself." In my mind, it was a win-win. If God didn't help me, my pastor would. *So, what do I have to lose?*

Remember, I was a baby in Christ and didn't understand it all, but I did remember the lesson he taught about paying ten percent of your gross earnings in obedience. I paid my tithes that Sunday, and when I went to the mailbox on Monday after work, there was a check in there. Someone had turned my name in months earlier for money that was being given to single parents as a one-time assistance payment that year. That check was not only enough to pay the electric bill, but it was also enough to fill my tank with gas and buy groceries. I was so excited! I even went out and bought some hamburger meat because I had extra money. Normally, I only bought chicken because it was cheaper. Hamburger meat was a luxury!

That was many years ago, and no matter how hard times got, I never put God on the back burner. Tithes first, and then everything else after that, and to this day, God has never let us down.

Pastor will be greatly missed, but he will remain in my heart forever. The valuable lessons he taught me continue to help me be the best me I can be.

My Guardian Angel

I was blessed to know a beautiful woman, inside and out, who made the greatest impact on my life. She was my angel.

Aunt Fanny was a slender woman who stood six feet tall and had the sweetest soul I had ever known. She taught me life lessons through actions more than words. She taught me how to forgive, live life to the fullest, and budget a dollar, but most of all, she taught me how to love.

She was always willing to do what she could when she could with the little that she had. In fact, I watched her give her last to others, even if they had more than she did. She was always a sucker for a sob story.

I felt unloved and slighted as a little girl, and she knew that because she lived close to us. There was even a point when she let me and my baby sister, Renee, live with her. Every night, she made us get on our knees and tell "The Man" about our day. Her rule was no matter what happened that day, tell God about it. Then, go to bed, forget about it, and have sweet dreams.

We stayed with Aunt Fanny for a over a year, and those were good times. She was going to keep us permanently. However, Mommie Dearest realized she couldn't file taxes with us as dependents if we didn't live at her address. So, we had to go back, back to a place where we didn't matter.

It's very difficult to put into words and describe what Aunt Fanny meant to me and how she influenced me, but the word that comes to mind is LOVE. In her eyes, love was an action word. As far back as I can remember, she was always there for me, even if it was just to listen, offer some advice, or loan me twenty dollars so I could make it to payday. Whatever or whenever I was in need, she was willing.

Aunt Fanny loved to drink, and sometimes she could go overboard. However, it didn't matter how much she was under the influence. Her love never wavered. Because she chose to drink and live her life like she wanted to, she was judged and looked down on, but she didn't care. She kept it moving.

As she aged, she was diagnosed with cancer. The first time she beat it. She was in remission for a few years, but it came back and was worse the second time around.

Per the doctor's recommendation, her voice box had to be removed to save her life. Although she was unable to speak, she refused to even try the suggestions for alternative ways to speak. So, she wrote down what she wanted to say on a pad.

April 18, 1994, is a date that will forever stick in my mind. I accompanied her to a doctor's appointment, as I had done so many times before, but this time, the tone in the room was different. The doctor advised her that the cancer had spread and she had about ninety days to live. They informed her that they were going to write orders to admit her to the nursing home to keep her comfortable because there was nothing more they could do.

As I sat there, in shock and faith all at the same time, I told him point-blank, "No, she will not be admitted to a nursing home. My husband and I promised we would never do that, and we won't." He informed us that it was not advisable to care for her at home due to the fact that she would require twenty-four-hour care. I responded with one word, "Understood," and that was the end of that conversation.

After we got settled in the car for our drive home, I looked at her notepad. She had written a note to the doctor telling him, "No," because my husband and I were going to care for her. Seeing that brought tears to my eyes. At that moment, I knew that she knew we would keep our word.

Over the next three months, I cared for her, and my husband cared for our children. It was a challenging, twenty-four-hour job, but it was doable thanks to a couple of cousins who came by to give me relief here and there. Many times, in her own way of communicating, she would look at me with approving eyes, letting me know she appreciated what we were doing, and that gave me the strength to hang in there day after day. At one point, she grabbed my arm and pulled me down to her as her way of hugging me. At that moment, I knew the time was near for us to say goodbye. I simply responded by telling her, "I love you too."

I cried a lot during those last few weeks, and even though I tried not to let her see it, she always knew. One fateful day, she wrote me a note and said, "Stop being selfish and let me go." In my time of prayer, I had been praying for her healing on this side, but she was praying for her own healing on the heavenly side. She believed in the power of prayer, and so did I. We just wanted different results.

Back when she was going into surgery to have her voice box removed, she told me, "Don't cry for me because I have lived my life. I have done everything I wanted to do. I have gone where I wanted to go, cooked what I wanted to eat, and lived how I wanted to live. And now I have made peace with God, and I am ready for His will to be done. If I die on the table as the doctor predicted, I'm ready to go." I remembered that conversation and realized that I was being selfish; and I, too, began to pray God's will be done and that He help me accept His will because I couldn't imagine life without her.

Less than forty-eight hours later, we had to rush her to the hospital, where she was admitted. A week later, I watched her take her last breath. To this day, that was the hardest thing I ever had to do. I wanted it to be a bad dream, but I knew it was real.

I gave the hospital the name of the funeral home and called my husband to let him know she was gone. I then crawled into the bed with her until the funeral home arrived.

Prior to that day, I had never felt a sense of loss that deep. It left a permanent hole in my heart. The love we shared could not be described in words; it could only be understood through actions.

After her homegoing celebration, I grieved for months. I even moved back to our hometown to live in her house. At the time, I believed it would help me feel closer to her. However, I now know I will always be close to her because I carry her in my heart. Still, not one day goes by that I don't think about her.

In one of the last conversations we had before she became ill, she told me I must walk tall because she would not always be with me. She said I needed to learn how to stand on my own two feet, and if she thought I was falling short at any point, she would tell me, "You are not walking tall like I taught you." I took that advice that day but didn't apply it until years later because I didn't truly understand it. I depended on her when, as a believer, I was supposed to depend on God and ask Him to help me walk tall. But why would I do that when she was always available? So, when she passed, I spent a lot of time feeling sorry for myself. Eventually, as I worked through my grief, I had a talk with Jesus, and it was clear: He wants to be Number One. It was her time to go, but at the time, she was my crutch and my number one. God wasn't.

Although it has been twenty-four years since she passed, the love she showed and the lessons she taught me continue to live on. It is my desire to give others what she gave me, and I pray that her love will live on for generations to come.

Marriage is not a Fairy Tale

In a marriage, we encounter seasons of significant difficulties filled with heartache and pain. One might begin seeking direction or solutions to overcome and get through these painful times. However, Discovering there is no step-by-step process can leave little hope or assurance that we will make it through to the other side.

When Javier and I first got to know each other, we became friends, sharing everything openly and honestly. We laughed all the time and shared common interests. Whether we were just riding and looking at the country, going to get fried chicken, chilling at the lake, or having a random picnic, we enjoyed each other's company.

One day, we decided to perform an act that children had no business doing. There was no understanding that once it happened, there would be no turning back. The result of this act brought a child into the world when we were only children ourselves.

Coming from an abusive home, I had no life coping skills or understanding of what a "normal" life was like, and Javier came from a divorced home with trust and abandonment issues. Neither of us was old enough or mature enough to understand the capacity of the baggage each of us carried, and combined, we were destined for failure. *How could we possibly avoid creating a home filled with dysfunction?* The adult choices we made had serious consequences, and that, coupled with alcohol and a little "Mary Jane," was a recipe for disaster.

I was addicted to Javier and believed he was the missing piece to make me whole, and Javier was looking for something but couldn't find it at home. This became a vicious cycle of years of mental and emotional abuse.

Twenty years later, after a second chance at marriage, I discovered I was in love with an addict who loved his drink of choice and other women more than the woman chosen for him and the family we created. I learned the hard way that love is not always enough. Trust was lost again, and he was back to his old ways. Infidelity seemed to be part of his DNA.

I spent many nights wondering, *Can I survive this again?* I was living with a familiar stranger as he lived a double life.

Each day presented the same question: *Should I go, or should I stay?*

He didn't stop the negative behavior; he just got better at it, and I didn't think I could continue in the marriage any longer. The children were grown and gone, and I could no longer hide behind the excuse that I was staying for them. I needed to figure out why I believed this was okay.

One morning, Javier came to me and told me, "I don't love you, and I don't think I ever have." I was devastated. He had just confessed to being with another woman three years prior, and I forgave him. I tried even harder to make things work, and he said that was what he wanted as well. So, I spent the next three years walking on eggshells, trying to do everything to show love and forgiveness, hoping he would finally see my value and fight for our marriage.

Nevertheless, hearing this was the final straw. His statement threw me into a tailspin of depression, and I didn't think I could recover, not this time. I sat there, thinking about everything pertaining to dying, intentionally trying not to focus on anything good. *How did I keep allowing myself to get here again and again? Even if it was true, why would he say that to me? I'm his ride-or-die. I'm nothing without him, but obviously, he's something without me.*

I repeatedly asked him what was wrong with me, "Why don't you love me?" His answer was the same every time, "It's not you; it's me." That was not the first time I had heard that. He often told me I deserved better than him because I was such a good woman. Yet, I wanted to convince him with everything in me that no one was better for me. I told him no one could take his place. I only wanted him.

Then I thought, *Why would he value me when I didn't even value myself."* I realized I allowed him to treat me this way, and there were no consequences for his bad choices. So, why wouldn't he do it again and again?

In thinking back to the beginning of my life, I often wondered why I wasn't allowed to just starve to death so I could have avoided the life of pain I had experienced. I may not have had the answer, but it was clear that I was exceptional from day one, and nobody realized it, not even me. Not knowing my mother or which man presented was my father left me feeling like an outsider, like I had something to prove because of the choices of two adults.

I wanted to have the family I dreamed and fantasized about, but missing the bond of a mother-daughter relationship contributed to many of my choices and character flaws. I know I didn't qualify for a Mother of the Year award when it came to my own children, but the one thing I did was give each of them all the love I had in my heart to give.

As I sat in tears, trying to figure out what the point was, I had to be honest. It made perfect sense why I would be willing to do everything within my power to give my children what I never had: a parental relationship. At least they knew who their parents were. Even if we were estranged at times, our children knew what they were or were not working with.

Nevertheless, I was tired of trying, tired of giving, tired of loving, tired of forgiving, and yes, tired of living. I made the decision that I was done with life once again. No more tears, pain, or heartache. May God have mercy on my soul.

I went to the garage equipped with the "good good," a glass of water, and a nice outfit. I had it all figured out. I'd crank the car, put on my favorite smooth jazz station, and drop off to sleep, saying goodbye to this world and my painful life. Unfortunately for him, Javier would be the one to find me, the woman who gave him her best years and all the love she knew how to give even though he didn't want or love me. Well, now he can figure out how to live without me because I didn't know how I could live without him.

As you figured out, I'm sure, it wasn't my time. I woke up coughing and gagging and let that garage door up quickly to get some air and come to my senses. Obviously, death was not the answer or solution. It was time for me to leave this marriage and save my life.

The Value of Me

I completed the divorce paperwork for him and told him all he had to do was file the papers with the court, and he'd be rid of me and free in sixty-three days and moved out three weeks later. For the first time in my life, I lived alone. I know today that was not the right decision for me as I realized I wasn't missing out on anything. I was more miserable away from Javier than I was with him. No matter what I did, there was never peace, and I tried to fill the void in every way I could think of, but nothing worked. It was not the answer I was seeking.

Maybe I chose to love Javier so long ago that I knew nothing else. He was the one I loved, and changing my address or my name didn't change the way I felt. Even though his words hurt, I still wanted to be with him, but I wanted him to want to be with me and to love me back.

The one thing I didn't regret was getting the courage to move out even though he asked me to stay. Finally, he would see that I valued myself enough to not want to be where I wouldn't be loved or wasn't wanted for all the right reasons.

His solution to our separation was that we could be roommates. I thought, *You got to be done lost your mind! I can't be your roommate. Boy, I love you too much for that.*

I can be transparent today and admit that I wanted him to value me more than I valued myself. I thought that if he loved me like I desired, that would make me complete. However, the emptiness I felt was not his job to fill. It was there for a different purpose.

That chapter lasted five months, and it was hard, but I learned a lot about myself. I didn't want to go back because I was broken, but I also didn't want to stay in my current situation. So I made another major decision.

Since he didn't want me, it was time for me to divorce him again and get my maiden name back. I felt the need to reclaim my own identity. I planned to get as far away from him as possible because I knew if he chose to be with someone else, it would crush me far more than what I was feeling at the time.

After I was gone for about a month, he called me and told me, "I just want to say this, and then I'll let you go: I miss you, and I can't think of anyone else I want to grow old with but you." Then, he ended the call.

I cried for about forty-five minutes straight. *What does that mean? Did he mean what he said, or was he taking it back? What is he saying?* He was always a man of few words, and I am an analyzer, who wants to know who, what, when, where, and why. His words played constantly in my mind, but I knew I needed to keep moving forward.

Keep Moving Forward

I continued working on a plan to move as far away from Javier as possible. So, applied for a job I knew I didn't qualify for. It was in a different city, and I used it as a test to see if it would be a sign of some sort.

When I applied for the job, I understood that it required me to be in the office daily. However, based on my address at the time of application, I was denied the opportunity. It was assumed that I was unwilling to relocate since the job was three hours away, so they planned to select somebody else. However, when the manager reached out regarding the denial, I explained that I understood they did not pay for relocation, and I was still willing to come as soon as they needed me. I was then offered the position and asked to start in two weeks.

Talking about nervous energy, I didn't think that plan through too well. I was walking away from life as I knew it, years of relationships. I was broken, and most of the people in my life never noticed. At an early age, I learned to play the part, paint on the smile, and do what I had to do no matter what it took. So, that's just what I did.

The time away from Javier was rough. I had found a small house but could not afford a bed. When I left, Javier said I could take whatever I wanted, but I wanted nothing from him. He could keep it all: the car, the furniture, the memories. All of it. So, I put my clothes in a suitcase and left.

Once in my little house, I slept on the floor for the first two months. I rarely ate, worked long hours, and volunteered quite a bit at church. I tried to keep it business as usual.

I escaped back into my fantasy land, living as Sandy. Don't let anybody down. You gave your word. You must show up and do what is expected. How could someone that had it all together fall apart like this? The real question was, *How did I survive everything I was committed to without another nervous breakdown?*

His Love Never Fails

After weeks of going nonstop, I decided to have a talk with God. I told him I couldn't serve Him anymore: "You don't answer my prayers, and the Christian life is just not for me. I am tired of being hurt by Your people while being ignored by You. But before I walk away, I just want to thank You for caring for my family, healing my body, and giving me the strength to do what I do. I also thank You for how You showed up for my children and grandchildren in their time of need and for the good years You provided me." I went on for quite some time, to the point that I lost track of time. I then realized, *I have literally lost my mind!* God knew exactly where I was and how to snap me out of it.

I fell on my face and asked God to forgive me for walking away from my covering and for everything I did or said that was against His will. I asked Him to help me surrender to Him so I could find peace again.

He led me to call my brother in Christ, and he and his wife prayed for me and eventually anointed me at the altar. He encouraged me as I shared all that I had been going through over the past few months, and they didn't judge me. Instead, they loved me and continued to encourage me, reminding me that God's love never fails.

I was back on track again, but this time, I was different. I was not the same woman that left my husband that hot summer day. The next time I visited Javier, I told him I was moving out of town in two weeks. He informed me he didn't file the paperwork while I was away and then asked, "So, when are we moving?" He chose to pack up and walk away from life as he knew it, and that was when God restored our marriage. For the first time, we became one.

From Emptiness to Purpose

It's funny how you think you are looking for something, and it was right in your face the entire time. Javier made terrible choices because he didn't trust that I would hang in here with him, and there was nothing I could do to convince him otherwise. I was so empty inside that I wanted him to fit in this little box I thought our marriage was supposed to be, but that was not my decision to make.

One thing I failed to realize is you can't become one in a marriage as God intended until you are a whole person in God first. I thought I was loving Javier through God, but without realizing it, I made him my god. It is a lot of pressure to want someone to give you something they don't have the capacity to give because it's not their job to do so. We were not expected to last forty days, and thanks be to God that with His guidance, we have been married for over thirty years.

I had to understand that I didn't succeed at suicide because God had work for me to do. I had come to believe when I prayed for others, God would work miracles in their lives, but that it worked for everyone except me. I now know there were seeds sown in me at an early age that convinced me that I was nothing and that I deserved nothing good, and when that happens, without the Blood of Jesus, it is hard to overcome. Hurt people hurt people, but healed people help people, and that's exactly what I did. I found purpose.

Life Lessons

After all the ups and downs on this roller-coaster called life, I finally understood that more was required of me. From the day I was born, the enemy knew what God had planned for my life, and that is why he tried to kill me before my first birthday, but his plan failed.

At a young age, I lost my mother and then endured an abusive childhood, enticing me to look for love in all the wrong places. I became an unwed teenage mother, suffered a nervous breakdown, and was married and divorced by age thirty. It would have been easy to find comfort in drugs and alcohol or to choose death over life to escape the pain, and I tried both but failed. It was clear: God created me for His purpose, to glorify Him, and through it all, He was right there. It just took me a while to acknowledge His presence.

I was not created to be a trash can. Yet, I lived a life filled with betrayal, hurt, and neglect. I spent most of my life empty, trying to fill a void only God could fill. Everything I went through was required to humble and prepare me to receive the blessings He prepared specifically for me.

Reflecting on life's lessons taught me how to move from feeling empty to fulfilled. It served as a reminder that God did not make junk when He created me. I had to learn how to respect myself before I could expect anyone else to, and during that lesson, I learned that it's not how you start but how you finish. Ninety-nine and a half won't do. We must give it one hundred percent every day, every time.

I have grown to understand that my life is my responsibility. It is filled with both good and bad choices through which I can make my life better or worse. I can be a victor or a victim, but either way, it is my choice.

I also realized that everyone that comes into our lives is not meant to stay. Some have a reason, some for a season, and a precious few make the cut for a lifetime. When we hold on to what or who God is telling us to let go of, we become too heavy to soar to the level He purposed for us.

Ultimately, I discovered that the final step to a fulfilling life is to embrace the true meaning of love. I searched for love my entire life, even falling in love with the idea of love. I was willing to sacrifice everything, including my identity, hoping for someone to love me enough to fill the emptiness I felt inside. I later learned that the void created was reserved for the one, true, honest-to-goodness love of my life. Yes, you guessed it: God. His love had been there all along.

God is Love, and when we truly accept this love through the gift of salvation and forgiveness, we can develop a relationship filled with fellowship, honesty, and obedience that will lead us to never know emptiness again. When God chooses to use us, He gets the Glory. There is no sense of emptiness, sorrow, or sadness, but the remnant is joy unspeakable and a peace that passeth all understanding. We can do many good things inside and outside the church building, but only what we do for Christ will last.

"All their life in this world and all their adventures had only been the cover and the title page: now at last they were beginning Chapter One of the Great Story which no one on earth has read: which goes on forever: in which every chapter is better than the one before."
~ C.S. Lewis, The Last Battle

Epilogue

I pray our story will help others realize distractions in life are meant to trip us up. If the enemy can get the father out of the home or sow seeds of defeat in the mother, then he has access to destroy the seed to whom God has already assigned the anointing. But one thing I know is that what God has for you is for you, and even though it might have taken us longer to get where we are, by God's grace, we made it.

We are now living a happy, peaceful, and loving life. I have found the kind of peace that makes you happy from the inside out, not based on what kind of day you're having or the stuff you own, just the peace in knowing you are right where you are supposed to be at this time in this season.

I now know that my healing is tied to telling my story, and that is the main reason for sharing it, unapologetically. I had been empty most of my life, even after being saved, but I am grateful that God stepped in and gave me exactly what I needed. He walked me through the process in His time, forgave me when I sinned, and received me back with loving arms when I walked away from Him as though it never happened.

Now, my life is full of peace and joy every day. Even when discouragement and tough times invade my space, I'm okay because the void was filled by the Master, who placed it there in the first place. No matter what happens, He always makes it better than it was before.

Many times, we want a quick fix and don't want to go through trying times, but God wants us to trust Him in such a way that no matter what happens, we will know that we know that He is bigger than whatever the "IT" is. If we surrender all to Him, we can truly testify that the battle is not ours; it's the Lord's. We will let nothing separate us from the love of God.

We should be excited and thrilled about making heaven our home, but while we are here, let's enjoy a little piece of heaven right here on Earth!

If you are empty today, you do not have to stay that way. When we ask Him to come into our hearts, He will, but that's not enough. We have to be intentional about spending time with God in fellowship to build a relationship. He did His part; He died for us. Now, what are we willing to do for Him to prove we accept the life promised in Him.

To go higher in God and grow, we must stay close to Him. As we study His Word and learn His will for our lives, we will be able to turn to Him when (not if) relationships with others try to break us. Whether it be a spouse, a child, a parent, a boss, a friend, or even a stranger, we will know He has our best interest in mind. Sometimes God won't get rid of whatever is bothering us right away, but He will provide the strength for us to endure it and have peace during the storm.

Be encouraged today! Hang in there, and don't give up. There is still more that God requires of us, and everything we need to accomplish His will for our lives is within us. If we are willing to put in the work, God is willing to take care of us, as He has shown us time and time again. Let's do what we can and let God do what we can't!

Surrender today to His perfect will, and remember, when you pray, don't worry – God's got you. He promises to never leave us nor forsake us and to supply all our needs according to his riches in glory.

Next time you feel overwhelmed as you serve God's people, ask yourself, "Am I doing church work or the work of the church? Trust me, there is a difference. Today, I am a witness that when God is in control, and you give yourself to Him, it is all good because it is all God!

As I close this chapter of my life in preparation for my next project, I know I am being led to continue to help others. What is it that your heart desires? Choose God, seek and serve Him, and keep Him first in everything you do. Then, watch Him bring it to fruition.

Jesus told us, "Be of good cheer, for I have overcome the world." Everything we need to succeed and walk into our destiny is within us. What God has for me is for me, and what he has for you is for you. I can do nothing with your purpose, and you can do nothing with mine. If we understand our place, stay in it, and follow God; nothing will be impossible when we believe!

To God be the glory for all the things He has done; and may blessings, peace, joy, grace, forgiveness (*you get the point*) be unto you!

About the Author

Elizabeth Carter is an encourager, mentor, and certified life coach who has experienced many ups and downs in this game called life. Yet no matter what, she has continued to fight the good fight and press on.

Mrs. Carter is filled with the imagination, experience, inspiration, and tenacity required to write. As a passionate author, her stories are intended to encourage, inspire, and help others on their journey to live life on their terms.

Her desire to tell this story was conceived over thirty years ago, a vision that would continue to grow inside her throughout all those years. This vision has finally come to term and is being pushed out and delivered. Although long overdue, every step of the journey has been purposed for this time and season.

Mrs. Carter loves reading, music, and fellowshipping with family and friends. She is the mother of four children and married to the love of her life.

Made in United States
Troutdale, OR
07/18/2023

11392823R00072